# 500

## pies & tarts

# 500

## pies & tarts

the only pies and tarts compendium you'll ever need

Rebecca Baugniet

SELLERS
PUBLISHING

A Quintet Book

Published by Sellers Publishing, Inc.
161 John Roberts Road, South Portland, Maine 04106
For ordering information:
(800) 625-3386 Toll Free
(207) 772-6814 Fax
Visit our Web site: www.rsvp.com • E-mail: rsp@rsvp.com

President and Publisher: Ronnie Sellers
Publishing Director: Robin Haywood
Managing Editor: Mary Baldwin
Senior Editor: Megan Hiller

ISBN: 978-1-56906-984-4
QUIN.FHP

This book was designed and produced by
Quintet Publishing Limited
6 Blundell Street
London N7 9BH
United Kingdom

Library of Congress Control Number: 2007921682

Editor: Marianne Canty
Art Editor: Dean Martin
Designer: Graham Saville
Photographer: Ian Garlick
Home Economist: Wendy Sweetser

10 9 8 7 6 5 4 3 2 1

Manufactured in Singapore by Pica Digital Pte Ltd.
Printed in China by SNP Leefung Printers Ltd.

# contents

# introduction

Few things in life are as inviting as the smell of a fresh-baked pie coming out of the oven, and what could be more satisfying than serving up a culinary masterpiece that you have created yourself? Pies and tarts take on many incarnations; they can contain sweet or savory fillings, have a top crust or be open-faced, may be served à la mode or handheld. In some cases, they can be quickly assembled, while in others they are the result of several stages of baking and preparation. In either case, nothing is as well appreciated as a home-baked pastry. The origin of pies dates back to ancient Egypt, when ingredients such as nuts and honey were wrapped in a pastrylike confection. Well-liked by the Greeks, who prepared the pastry mainly with meat or fish, it was then adopted by the Romans when they conquered Greece. The Romans adapted recipes they had brought home to incorporate local ingredients, resulting in many of the variations we find today — the most famous one being pizza. From Italy, pies were introduced all over Europe, and were finally brought to America by British settlers, where they became further transformed by a new selection of ingredients.

The word "pie," according to the *Oxford English Dictionary*, is believed to have been named "by association with the magpie, after its tendency to collect miscellaneous articles." With only a few exceptions, all the pies in this book include some sort of pastry, be it a shell, a lid, or both. Unlike the pies, the tarts offered here are limited to baked pastry crusts with low sides, encasing different ingredients without any lid. Made popular in France, these elegant pastries never fail to please. Whichever recipe you try first, enjoy this time-honored process, and you are sure to enjoy the results.

# equipment

You need only a few basic pieces of equipment to make most pies and tarts.

### measuring cups & spoons
Baking is an exact science, so correct measuring equipment is essential. Always use calibrated measuring cups and proper measuring spoons. Flour should be spooned into measuring cups for accurate measurements.

### mixing bowls & electric mixers
A variety of mixing bowls is essential in the baker's kitchen. You will need a large bowl in which to make pastry. Medium bowls are useful when letting fruit fillings release their juices, and small bowls are necessary for melting butter and chocolate, separating eggs, and mixing small quantities. Electric mixers are helpful when extended beating is required, as with meringue and whipped cream. You may find that using a stand mixer will allow you to perform other tasks in the kitchen while the beating is occurring.

### spatulas, knives & pie servers
Spatulas are essential for scraping filling out of mixing bowls, smoothing filling, folding ingredients into delicate mixtures, and arranging meringue or whipped cream on top of fillings. They can also be used for sliding between rolled-out pastry and rolling surfaces if pastry is sticking. Have a variety of spatulas on hand when baking — rubber, metal, flat, and offset. Sharp knives are necessary for making a smooth cut in pies and tarts. For the cleanest cut, wipe your knife with a clean, damp paper towel between slices. A pie server is always useful for removing the perfect slice from a pie plate or tart pan.

### sieves, graters & zesters

You will need a large sieve for sifting dried ingredients such as flour and straining some fillings. Use a small sieve for dusting confectioners' sugar or cocoa over the baked pies and tarts. A coarse grater is necessary for grating cheese and a fine grater, such as a Microplane, is useful for grating fine citrus zest or ginger. If a fine grater is not available, a zester can be used. The rind can then be finely chopped, if necessary.

### rolling pins & boards

Many models of rolling pin are available, so choose one that suits your needs and which you find comfortable to work with. The preferred model among bakers remains the wooden French rolling pin with tapered ends. However, in a pinch, you can always use an empty wine bottle. Marble pastry boards offer the smoothest, coolest surface on which to roll out pastry, but a large wooden board or even a well-cleaned countertop will also work nicely.

### pie plates & tart pans

Most of the pies and tarts in this book are made in a 9-in. (23-cm.) pie plate, or 9-, 10-, or 11-in. (23-, 25-, 28-cm.) tart pans with removable bases. Pie plates are available in glass, aluminum, and ceramic. Glass distributes heat evenly, and allows you to see how the pie shell is browning. Aluminum pans are reputed to make a flakier crust, while ceramic plates are the obvious choice for attractive presentation. Ceramic plates will sometimes require a slightly longer baking time, so consult the manufacturer's directions. Muffin pans or individual 4-in. (10-cm.) tartlet pans are used for the mini pies and tartlets. Barquette molds are small boat-shaped molds useful for making appetizers. Rectangular and square tart pans are also available, and can be substituted for the circular pans in this book. However, the volume of the filling must be adjusted accordingly.

### cookie sheets, parchment paper, pie weights & plastic wrap

Cookie sheets are useful for ease of transfer from counter to oven, as well as for catching any drips that may leak from juicier fillings. Line cookie sheets with parchment paper for easy clean-up. Parchment paper is also necessary for prebaking. Pie weights are available at kitchen stores and can be found in ceramic or metal. Dried beans or rice may also be substituted for baking weights. Plastic wrap is necessary for wrapping discs of dough to chill in the refrigerator. Also, sandwiching pastry dough between two sheets of plastic wrap can make rolling easier. Peel off the plastic wrap for transfer to the pie plate.

### timers

When baking pies and tarts, timing is crucial. Either use the timer on your oven or invest in an inexpensive, accurate digital timer.

### wire racks

After baking, most pies and tarts should be transferred to a wire rack to cool.

### other equipment

Food processors can be used for mixing pastry dough, making cookie crumbs, and grinding nuts. They are also useful for fillings that require puréed ingredients. Pastry blenders are handheld metal utensils that facilitate the blending of flour and fats. A pastry brush is necessary for applying glazes and sealing some piecrusts. Whisks are also essential for whisking certain fillings as they cook.

# ingredients

While pastry itself calls on only a few ingredients — fat, flour, and liquid to bind, the fillings for these pastry cases can be as plain or exotic, as mild or aromatic as you choose. Try to use the freshest ingredients whenever possible. Organic ingredients that have been produced free of any chemicals or pesticides will always result in the tastiest baked goods.

### butter, shortening & lard
Butter and vegetable shortening are the two main fats used in the pastry recipes in this book. Unsalted butter is used in all the recipes, unless otherwise specified. Butter is the fat that provides pastry with its rich flavor, while vegetable shortening is used to create a light and flaky crust. Look for trans-fat-free vegetable shortenings in natural food stores. Lard is the fat rendered from pork and is naturally trans-fat free. While it is not used in the recipes in this book, it can be used to replace any portion of the fat content in the basic crust. Experiment with different fat combinations to find your own favorite pastry flavor and texture.

### sugars & other sweeteners
Granulated sugar is used for all recipes, unless otherwise specified. Confectioners' sugar, made with powdered granulated sugar and a small quantity of cornstarch, is used in whipped cream as well as assorted pie fillings. Brown sugar should always be packed when measured. Superfine and raw sugars can also be useful in baking — try sprinkling a coarse sugar such as demerara or turbinado over a top crust for a lovely finish to a fruit-filled pie. Other sweeteners, such as corn syrup, molasses, honey, and maple syrup, all lend their own distinctive flavors to various pie fillings.

### flour & flour alternatives

All-purpose flour is used in all recipes, unless otherwise specified. Whole-wheat flour can replace a portion of the all-purpose flour in the basic crust recipe; however, this can result in a slightly more brittle, fragile, and less flaky crust. Cornmeal is also used for a different flavor and texture, as are finely ground nuts. Finely ground cookies or crackers are used in the crumb crusts.

### eggs

Large eggs are used in all the recipes, unless otherwise specified. Eggs are most easily separated when cold. For best results when making meringue, use egg whites at room temperature and avoid using plastic bowls, which can retain a greasy film. Certain pie fillings contain meringue that has not been cooked, and should therefore be avoided by pregnant or nursing women, as well as babies under 12 months. Pasteurized egg whites can be found in some grocery stores, and may be used as a safe alternative.

### thickeners & gelatin

The two main kinds of thickener are cornstarch and flour. Cornstarch results in a silky texture with a translucent sheen, as in lemon curd. Instant tapioca can also be used as a substitute for cornstarch. Flour is used in small quantities to thicken fruit fillings without altering the texture of the filling. Gelatin is an unsweetened and unflavored product used to set liquid fillings. Gelatin must be sprinkled over cold water or other liquid to soften for several minutes before being added to a hot mixture to dissolve.

# prepared piecrusts

Many varieties of prepared pastry are available at supermarkets. Whether you are a novice baker with a fear of making pastry, or an experienced baker in a rush, these products allow you to skip a step and still achieve a satisfying homemade result.

### store-bought pie shells

Prepared pie pastry comes in several forms and is widely available in supermarket frozen and refrigerated aisles. The three main types are ready to roll, prerolled and ready to bake in an aluminum pie plate, and prerolled and folded in quarters. The first allows you to roll out the pastry yourself and line your own pie plate. The second requires no preparation at all — simply fill and bake. The third only requires unfolding the pastry and placing it in your own pie plate. When choosing a prepared pastry, check ingredient lists to find the one that best suits your tastes. Whichever you decide on, be sure to follow the package instructions for baking guidelines.

### puff pastry

Prepared puff pastry and puff pastry patty shells (vol-au-vents) are also widely available in supermarket frozen aisles, but it is worthwhile seeking out the all-butter varieties that can often be found in smaller gourmet food stores and some bakeries.

### phyllo dough

Phyllo sheets are widely available in supermarket frozen aisles. They must be fully thawed before using, so make sure you buy your package at least a day before you need it. Keep your stack of phyllo sheets moist while you are working by placing a clean, damp kitchen towel over the ones you aren't using.

**crumb crusts**

Graham cracker and chocolate wafer crumb crusts can also be found, usually in supermarket baking aisles. Prebake according to package instructions.

## other ingredients & flavorings

Fruit is one of the main ingredients in pie making. While fresh fruit in season will result in the most intense flavors, frozen is an acceptable substitute. Simply measure the fruit while it is still frozen, then allow the fruit to thaw and drain before adding it to the other filling ingredients. Try to use unwaxed fruit in any pie that uses the skin, zest, or rind of a fruit. Cream of tartar, usually found in supermarket baking aisles with herbs and spices, is a by-product of wine fermentation that stabilizes egg whites and prevents them from deflating. Vanilla extract is a common and popular flavor in baking. You can make your own vanilla extract by slitting 4 or 5 vanilla beans and placing them in a Mason jar with 2 cups of brandy or bourbon. Place the jar in a dark place and let stand for at least 2 weeks before using.

# pies & tarts basics

While pastry may have the reputation of being too time-consuming or difficult to tackle, once you have succeeded in producing a beautiful pie or tart you will see what a misconception this actually is. Most pie and tart recipes are easily divided into a series of small tasks, each one taking no more than a few minutes. Choose a recipe according to your needs. If you are in a hurry, you may wish to skip a step by using a store-bought pie shell or look for one of our quick and easy recipes. These are the pies and tarts that can be prepared and baked in 1 hour or less and are designated by a **clock icon**. Recipes with a **quick and easy shortcut** suggest components that can be easily replaced using store-bought products. Recipes with a **spoon icon** indicate that they are **easy to assemble** but may require longer baking, setting, or chilling times.

### preparing to bake

Make sure to read through the recipe well before you plan to bake, to establish how long you will need to get from start to finish as well as to verify that you have all the necessary ingredients on hand. Baking involves using many kitchen surfaces for all the various steps — making and rolling out the pastry, preparing the filling, cooling pie shells, etc. — so it is always a good idea to start with a clean kitchen.

### making pastry

Once you have read through the recipe and have all the ingredients on hand, you are ready to start! The oven temperatures are always listed at the beginning of the instructions, but it is not always necessary to begin preheating immediately. As long as you turn your oven on 10 minutes before the pie or tart goes into the oven, it should be hot enough. If you are uncertain about your oven's accuracy, use an oven thermometer, sold in hardware stores or kitchen stores.

Cold ingredients will result in a flakier crust, so be sure to use chilled butter and shortening. You want little particles of fat wrapped in layers of flour, as this is what will create the flaky pockets associated with a tender crust. The key to making good pastry is to work quickly and confidently, keeping your ingredients cold and not overworking the pie dough. The more you make pastry, the easier it will be for you to recognize the best consistency for the perfect pie crust. Bear in mind that flour will hold different levels of moisture in different weather, so add only as much liquid as is necessary to hold the dough together.

The recipes in this book give instructions for making pastry by hand, but it is possible to achieve the same results with a food processor. Simply pulse the flour and salt to combine, then add the chilled fat and process until the mixture resembles damp sand or coarse breadcrumbs. Sprinkle the liquid ingredients over the mixture and pulse until the dough begins to stick together. Proceed as with the hand method.

### prebaking, baking blind & fully baked crusts

Different pies and tarts require different baking techniques for the crust. Prebaking is most often used to prevent a soggy crust and partially bake a pie shell that will return to the oven only for a short period of time, as with a lemon meringue pie. Baking blind is the technique used for most tart shells, and involves lining the tart shell with parchment paper and filling it with weights (pie weights can be purchased in kitchen shops), dried beans, or rice. This is a crucial step in tart making, as it will prevent the pastry shell from shrinking or becoming soggy when filled. Fully baked crusts are for pie and tart shells that will not return to the oven once filled, and require slightly longer prebaking to ensure a nice brown crust. In all cases, chill the pie or tart shell for 10 minutes in the freezer before placing it on the middle shelf of your preheated oven.

### preparing the filling

Once again, it is important to read through the recipe to know when to prepare the filling. Certain fillings, such as chiffons and mousses, need to set in the pie crust, so it is best to prepare these once the pie shell has cooled to room temperature, at least 4 hours before serving time. Some fillings, like the pastry cream and lemon curd, can be prepared up to 3 days ahead of time, and kept refrigerated until they are needed. Cream fillings will result in a soggy crust if left to sit for too long. For this reason, it is best to fill the crust as close to serving time as possible. In all cases, you will achieve the best results and prevent a soggy crust if your filling is the same temperature as your pie shell.

### storing

Pie dough can be prepared ahead of time and stored in the refrigerator or freezer. Well-wrapped discs of pie dough will keep in the refrigerator for up to 3 days. For storing in the freezer, roll out the pie dough and line a pie plate. Double wrap in plastic wrap or place in a sealed freezer bag and store for up to 2 months. Frozen pie crusts can be filled or baked directly from the freezer.

### decorating pies & tarts

Pies and tarts can be decorated in many ways. Use the following suggestions, or be creative and come up with your own signature way of finishing a pie crust!

### single crusts

Single crusts are crimped before being chilled. Use the tines of a fork to press lightly around the edge for an easy, classic look. Use your left index finger to press the edge of the dough in while your right thumb and index finger push the dough out around your left index finger to create a fluted edge. Use small decorative cutters to make shapes out of pastry scraps.

Brush the edge of the crust with water and press down lightly on your shapes to seal. Or, wrap long ribbons of scrap dough together for a braid or twist edge. Again, brush the crust with water before placing the twist of pastry on top to seal.

## double crusts

Once you have placed the top crust over your filling, trim the edge to a 1/2-in. (1.5-cm.) overhang. Techniques for sealing the seam include folding the bottom crust over the edge of the top crust and crimping, or tucking the top crust under the edge of the bottom crust and crimping. Experiment to find your own favorite method. For a plain top, simply cut slits for steam to escape. For a crunchy top, glaze with your choice of lightly beaten egg, milk, or water and sprinkle coarse sugar on top. For a decorative top, use small cutters to cut out shapes before you place the top crust over the filling.

## lattice top

An easy lattice top can be made by simply cutting the rolled-out pie crust into 1-in. (2.5-cm.) strips, using a fluted pastry cutter, sharp knife, or pizza cutter. Arrange 5 to 7 strips across the filling, spacing evenly. Rotate the pie by 1/4 turn and place the other 5 to 7 slices across. Trim the excess from the edges of the lattice strips. Fold the bottom crust over the edges, and press down to seal and crimp. Glaze with lightly beaten egg for a glossy finish if desired. A classic woven lattice top can be made by cutting the rolled-out pie crust as above. Arrange 5 to 7 strips across the filling, spacing evenly. Rotate the pie by 1/4 turn and begin weaving in the other 5 to 7 slices, over and under the first set of strips. It may be easier to prepare the woven lattice top on a flat surface and then carefully transfer it to the pie. Trim the excess from the edges of the lattice strips. Fold the bottom crust over the lattice edge, and press down to seal and crimp. Glaze with lightly beaten egg for a glossy finish if desired.

# basic crust

This is the perfect crust for fruit-based pies as well as for savory tarts.

2 cups all-purpose flour
1/8 tsp. salt
1/2 cup vegetable shortening
1/2 cup cold unsalted butter

1 large egg
2 tsp. white vinegar
2 tbsp. ice-cold water

Combine the flour and salt in a large mixing bowl. Cut the vegetable shortening and butter into small chunks and add to the flour mixture. Using a pastry blender or two knives in a criss-crossing motion, blend the butter and shortening into the flour mixture until it has the consistency of damp sand, with a few pea-sized pieces of butter and shortening remaining. Using a fork or wire whisk, beat the egg with the vinegar and water. Slowly pour the egg mixture over the flour, stirring only until the mixture is moist. The dough should stick together and be able to hold the form of a ball. Divide the dough into two balls and wrap each one in plastic wrap. Smooth each ball of dough with a rolling pin so it forms a flat disc that fills the corners of the plastic wrap. Chill in the refrigerator for a minimum of half an hour. (If it has been chilled for a long time, it may need to soften slightly before use.) To roll out the crust, unwrap one disc and place on a lightly floured surface. Roll the dough from the center of the disc to the edge, until the crust is the desired thickness (usually 1/8 in./ 3 mm. thick) and at least 1 in. (2.5 cm.) wider than the pie plate. If the dough is sticking to the rolling pin, try placing a sheet of plastic wrap over it and then rolling it out. Remove the plastic wrap and transfer the crust into the pie plate by rolling it onto the rolling pin and then positioning it over the pie plate. If the crust is sticking to the rolling surface, carefully separate it by sliding a sharp knife or metal spatula between the crust and the rolling surface. Carefully press the dough into the pie plate. If any cracks appear during the transfer, use lightly floured fingers to push the seams back together. For single-crust pies, crimp the edge decoratively, using your fingers or fork tines. Dough can be stored in the refrigerator for up to 3 days. If you wish to freeze the crust, first roll out the dough and line your pie plate. Once the crust is frozen, gently remove it from the pie plate and freeze in a large freezer bag for up to 3 months. Makes enough for two 8- or 9-in. (20- or 23-cm.) pie crusts.

> **QUICK & EASY SHORTCUT:** Grate chilled pie dough into the middle of a 9-in. (23-cm.) pie plate. Press evenly into the plate, beginning in the center and working outward, until the crust covers the bottom and sides of the dish. Crimp the edge decoratively.

## basic crust variations

**citrus crust:** prepare the basic crust, adding the zest of 1 lemon (1 to 2 teaspoons) to the flour mixture, and using 2 teaspoons of lemon juice in place of the white vinegar.

**whole-wheat crust:** prepare the basic crust, reducing the all-purpose flour to 1 cup and adding 1 cup whole-wheat flour.

**cinnamon crust:** prepare the basic crust, adding 1 teaspoon of cinnamon to the flour mixture.

**cheddar crust:** prepare the basic crust, increasing the flour to 2 1/2 cups and adding 1 tablespoon of granulated sugar to the flour mixture. Reduce the vegetable shortening to 1/3 cup. Once the butter and shortening have been blended, cut in 1 cup of grated aged cheddar cheese until just incorporated. Increase the ice water as necessary.

**cornmeal crust:** prepare the basic crust, reducing the all-purpose flour to 1 1/2 cups. Add 1/2 cup yellow cornmeal to the flour mixture.

# basic sweet crust

This is the crust to use in a shallow, fluted tart pan. It is ideal for custard-filled tarts.

1 cup all-purpose flour
1/8 tsp. salt
1/4 cup granulated sugar

1/2 cup cold unsalted butter
1 large egg yolk
1-2 tbsp. ice-cold water

Combine the flour, salt, and sugar in a medium bowl. Cut the butter into small chunks and add to the flour mixture. Using a pastry blender or two knives in a criss-crossing motion, blend the butter into the flour mixture until it has the consistency of damp sand, with a few pea-sized pieces remaining.

Using a fork or wire whisk, beat the egg yolk with the cold water. Slowly pour the egg mixture over the flour, stirring only until the mixture has become moistened. The dough should stick together and be able to hold the form of a ball. Cover the ball with plastic wrap. Smooth the ball of dough with a rolling pin so it forms a flat disc that fills the corners of the plastic wrap. Chill in the refrigerator for a minimum of half an hour. (If it has been chilled for a long time, it may need to soften slightly at room temperature before use.)

To roll out the piecrust, unwrap the disc and place on a lightly floured rolling surface. Roll the dough from the center of the disc to the edge, until the crust is the desired thickness and 1 in. (2.5 cm.) wider than the pie pan it will fit. If the dough is sticking to the rolling pin, try placing a sheet of plastic wrap over it and then rolling it out. Remove the plastic wrap and transfer the crust into the pie pan by rolling it onto the rolling pin and then positioning it over the pie pan. Carefully press the dough into the pie pan. If any cracks appear during the transfer, use lightly floured fingers to push the seams back together. If you cannot transfer the entire piece of dough at once, do not panic — this dough patches easily. Simply cover the base of the tart pan with the main portion of the dough, and use the scraps to cover the sides. Trim the excess from the edge of the tart crust.

> **QUICK & EASY SHORTCUT:** Cut the disc into 1/8-in. (0.3-cm.) slices and arrange them on the bottom and along the sides of the tart pan. Press to join the pieces and distribute the dough evenly over the surface of the pan. Trim the excess from the edge of the crust.

## basic sweet crust variations

**vanilla sweet crust:** prepare the basic recipe, adding 1/2 teaspoon vanilla extract to the egg yolk and water mixture.

**almond sweet crust:** prepare the basic recipe, reducing the amount of all-purpose flour to 3/4 cup and adding 1/4 cup finely ground almonds to the flour mixture.

**hazelnut sweet crust:** prepare the basic recipe, reducing the amount of all-purpose flour to 3/4 cup and adding 1/4 cup finely ground hazelnuts to the flour mixture.

**chocolate sweet crust:** prepare the basic recipe, adding 2 tablespoons unsweetened Dutch-process cocoa to the flour mixture.

**lemon sweet crust:** prepare the basic recipe, adding the zest of 1 lemon to the flour mixture.

**confectioners' sugar sweet crust:** prepare the basic recipe, replacing the 1/4 cup sugar with 1/4 cup confectioners' sugar.

# basic crumb crust

This is a quick and easy crust to make, and is well suited for cream pies and frozen pies.

1 cup graham cracker crumbs (aprox. 16 graham crackers ground in a food processor)

1/4 cup unsalted butter, melted
1 tbsp. granulated sugar or honey
1 tbsp. all-purpose flour

Preheat the oven to 350°F (175°C). Combine all the ingredients until they are well blended. Press evenly into a 9-in. (23-cm.) pie plate, beginning in the center and working outward, until the crust covers the bottom and sides of the plate. If you find your fingers are too sticky to do the job nicely, wrap them in plastic wrap and then proceed. Alternatively, you can dust your fingers with sugar as required. Bake for 10 to 15 minutes.

## basic crumb crust variations

**chocolate wafer crumb crust:** prepare the basic crumb crust recipe, replacing the graham cracker crumbs with 1 cup chocolate wafer cookie crumbs.

**gingersnap crumb crust:** prepare the basic crumb crust recipe, replacing the graham cracker crumbs with 1 cup gingersnap cookie crumbs.

**light crumb crust:** prepare the basic crumb crust recipe, reducing the amount of unsalted butter to 1 tablespoon and adding 1 large egg white to the crumb mixture.

**shortbread crumb crust:** prepare the basic crumb crust recipe, replacing the graham crackers with 1 cup shortbread crumbs.

# basic pastry cream

This useful pastry cream can be made up to 1 day ahead.

1/2 cup granulated sugar
2 large eggs, lightly beaten
1 large egg yolk, lightly beaten
2 tbsp. cornstarch

1 cup whole milk
1/2 cup whipping cream
2 tsp. vanilla extract

Combine the sugar, eggs, egg yolk, and cornstarch in a medium bowl. Set aside. Place the milk and cream in a double boiler or heavy-bottomed medium saucepan over low heat. Bring to a simmer and remove from the heat. Slowly whisk the hot milk and cream into the sugar mixture. When smooth, return to the saucepan and cook over medium heat, whisking constantly, until the mixture begins to thicken. Bring the thickened mixture to a boil and cook for 1 minute, still whisking constantly. Remove from the heat and stir in the vanilla. Place plastic wrap or parchment paper on the surface to prevent a skin from forming and chill in the refrigerator until needed, or for a minimum of 3 hours.

## basic pastry cream variations

**citrus-scented pastry cream:** prepare the basic recipe, adding the zest of 1 lemon or 1 orange with the vanilla. Reduce the vanilla extract to 1 teaspoon.

**cinnamon pastry cream:** prepare the basic recipe, adding 1 teaspoon ground cinnamon with the vanilla. Reduce vanilla extract to 1 teaspoon.

**rum-scented pastry cream:** prepare the basic recipe, adding 1 tablespoon rum with the vanilla extract.

**almond-scented pastry cream:** prepare the basic recipe, reducing the vanilla extract to 1 teaspoon and adding 1 teaspoon almond extract.

# basic cream cheese filling

This filling can be used as an alternative to pastry cream in fresh fruit tarts.

1 cup (one 8-oz. package) cream cheese,
   softened
1/4 cup confectioners' sugar

2 tsp. fresh lemon juice
1/2 cup whipping cream

Combine the first 3 ingredients in a large bowl. Using an electric mixer, beat on medium until smooth. Add the whipping cream and continue beating until the mixture is light and fluffy. Makes enough to fill a 9-in. (23-cm.) tart shell.

### basic cream cheese variations

**mascarpone filling:** prepare the basic recipe, replacing the cream cheese with mascarpone cheese. Omit the lemon juice and add 4 oz. melted and cooled white chocolate.

**crème fraiche filling:** prepare the basic recipe, replacing the lemon juice with 1/2 tsp. vanilla extract. Replace the whipping cream with 1/2 cup crème fraiche.

# basic whipped cream

Basic whipped cream can be folded into a pie filling, used as a topping, or simply used as a garnish. For best results, always use chilled whipping cream and a chilled metal mixing bowl.

**1 cup whipping cream**                **1 tbsp. confectioners' sugar**

Using an electric mixer, beat the cream in a large bowl until frothy. Add the sugar and continue beating until soft peaks form and the cream has doubled in volume. Do not overbeat. Whipped cream can be prepared up to 4 hours in advance.

## basic whipped cream variations

**vanilla-scented whipped cream:**  prepare the basic recipe, adding 1/2 teaspoon vanilla extract with the sugar.

**bailey's-scented whipped cream:**  prepare the basic recipe, adding 1 tablespoon Bailey's Irish Cream with the sugar.

# basic meringue

Meringue can be folded into pie fillings or used as a topping. For best results, use egg whites at room temperature. Meringue can be difficult to make on very humid days — if used to top a pie in this weather, the meringue will "weep" (small droplets will form on the surface).

3 large egg whites
1/4 tsp. cream of tartar

1/3 cup granulated sugar

Using an electric mixer, beat the egg whites and cream of tartar in a large bowl until frothy. Add the sugar, a tablespoon at a time, and continue beating until soft peaks form. At this stage, watch carefully so you do not overbeat. Continue beating until the peaks become stiff — they will hold their shape when the beaters are lifted, drooping only slightly. The meringue must be used as soon as possible after it has been made, before it begins to deflate.

# basic sauces

## hot fudge sauce

12-oz. can evaporated milk
2 cups semisweet chocolate chips
1/2 cup granulated sugar

1 tbsp. unsalted butter
1 tsp. vanilla extract

Combine the milk, chocolate chips, and sugar in a heavy-based saucepan. Cook over medium heat, stirring constantly, until the chocolate chips have melted and the mixture comes to a boil. Remove from the heat and add the butter and vanilla. Stir until smooth. Hot fudge sauce can be kept, refrigerated, for 1 month.

## butterscotch sauce

2/3 cup evaporated milk
1/4 cup light corn syrup
1 cup light brown sugar, packed
1 cup granulated sugar

pinch of salt
2 tbsp. unsalted butter
1 tsp. vanilla extract

Combine the milk, corn syrup, sugars, and salt in a heavy-based saucepan. Cook over low heat, stirring often, until the mixture thickens, about 20 minutes. Remove from the heat and add the butter and vanilla. Stir until smooth. Butterscotch sauce can be kept, refrigerated, for 1 month.

## caramel sauce

1/2 cup unsalted butter
1 cup light brown sugar

1/2 cup whipping cream

Melt the butter over low heat in heavy-based saucepan. Add the sugar and cream. Continue cooking over low heat, stirring constantly, until the sugar has dissolved and the mixture is smooth. Remove from the heat. Caramel sauce can be kept, refrigerated, for 1 week.

## kiwi coulis

6 kiwis, peeled

juice of 1 lemon

Using a handheld blender or a food processor, purée the kiwis. Press the purée through a fine sieve and stir in the lemon juice. Refrigerate any remaining kiwi coulis for up to 3 days.

### raspberry coulis

1 cup granulated sugar
1/2 cup water

1 1/2 cups fresh or frozen raspberries

Combine the sugar and water in a small saucepan and cook, stirring frequently, until the sugar has dissolved. Remove from the heat and cool. Using a handheld blender or a food processor, purée the raspberries. Add the sugar syrup and stir until well combined. Strain the mixture through a fine sieve. Refrigerate any remaining raspberry coulis for up to 3 days.

# basic toppings

### pecan crunch topping

1 cup chopped pecans
1 tbsp. unsalted butter

pinch of salt

Make the pecan crunch topping by toasting the pecans in the butter with a pinch of salt. Cook over medium heat for 5 minutes, until the nuts start to turn golden.

### basic streusel topping

3/4 cup all-purpose flour
1/3 cup light brown sugar, packed
3 tbsp. granulated sugar

pinch of cinnamon
pinch of salt
6 tbsp. unsalted butter

To prepare the streusel topping, combine the flour, sugars, cinnamon, and salt in a medium bowl. Using your fingers, cut the butter into the flour mixture, until large clumps form.

### crunchy coconut topping
**1/2 cup sweetened flaked coconut**        **1/3 cup chopped macadamia nuts**

Combine 1/2 cup flaked coconut and 1/3 cup chopped macadamia nuts, pecans, or walnuts.

# basic glazes

### apricot jelly glaze
**1/4 cup apricot jelly or strained apricot jam**        **1 tsp. water**

Warm the apricot jelly in a small saucepan over low heat. Add the water and stir until smooth. Using a pastry brush, glaze the fruit.

### basic glaze variations

**red currant jelly:** prepare the basic recipe, replacing the apricot jelly with an equal quantity of red currant jelly.

**honey glaze**: prepare the basic recipe, replacing the apricot jelly with an equal quantity of honey.

# classic pies & tarts

These are the pies and tarts that never go out of
style. Handed down through generations of home
bakers, these timeless recipes are sure to become
favorites of yours as well.

# perfect apple pie

see variations page 48

This pie is at its best in the fall when made with fresh, local apples. However, you can enjoy it year-round with the different varieties of apples available at your supermarket.

1 recipe basic crust (page 18)
3/4 cup light brown sugar
1–2 tsp. lemon juice
1 tsp. cinnamon
pinch of salt

pinch of nutmeg
1 tbsp. all-purpose flour
6 McIntosh apples, peeled, cored,
    and sliced thinly
1 tbsp. unsalted butter

Preheat the oven to 425°F (220°C). Mix the sugar, lemon juice, cinnamon, salt, nutmeg, and flour together. Place the sliced apples in a medium bowl, pour the mixture over them, and toss gently to coat evenly.

Roll out half the quantity (one disc) of the pastry dough and line a 9-in. (23-cm.) pie plate. Tip the apples into the crust and dot with butter. Roll out the second disc of pastry dough. Put the top crust on the pie, crimp the edges, and make 4 to 6 slits in the crust. Bake for 10 minutes.

Lower the temperature to 350°F (175°C) and continue baking for 35 to 40 minutes, or until the crust is golden brown. Transfer to a wire rack and cool for 1 hour. Serve warm or at room temperature.

*Serves 6–8*

# lemon meringue pie

see variations page 49

This light and tart pie is the perfect way to end a special meal.

1/2 recipe basic crust (page 18)
1 cup granulated sugar
1/4 cup cornstarch
1/8 tsp. salt
1 1/4 cups warm water

1/4 cup fresh lemon juice
zest from 1 lemon
3 large egg yolks, lightly
    beaten
1 tbsp. unsalted butter

3 large egg whites
1/4 tsp. cream of tartar
1/2 tsp. vanilla extract
1/3 cup superfine sugar

Preheat the oven to 425°F (220°C). Roll out the pastry dough and line a 9-in. (23-cm.) pie plate. Prick the surface with a fork and prebake for 15 minutes. Cool on a wire rack. Lower the temperature to 350°F (175°C). Combine the granulated sugar, cornstarch, and salt in a double boiler. Over low heat, slowly whisk in the warm water. Then add the lemon juice and zest, egg yolks, and butter. Cook, whisking constantly, until the mixture comes to a boil and thickens. The lemon curd should mound when dropped from a spoon. Remove from the heat. Press a sheet of parchment paper onto the surface to prevent a skin from forming, and cool thoroughly.

Beat the egg whites, cream of tartar, and vanilla with an electric mixer. When the egg whites become foamy, begin adding the superfine sugar a tablespoon at a time. Continue beating until stiff peaks form. Pour the cooled lemon curd into the cooled piecrust. Top with the meringue and bake for 12 to 15 minutes, until the meringue peaks turn golden brown. Transfer to a wire rack and cool before serving.

*Serves 6–8*

# glazed fruit tart

see variations page 50

This classic tart can be found in French patisseries around the world. Prepare your tart shell and pastry cream ahead of time, and you can assemble this tart in minutes.

1 recipe basic sweet crust (page 20)
1 large egg, lightly beaten
1 recipe basic pastry cream (page 23)

3 cups assorted fresh fruits, such as thinly
    sliced pears, plums, peaches, kiwis, berries,
    and grapes
1/4 cup apricot jelly or strained apricot jam
1 tsp. water

Preheat the oven to 400°F (200°C). Roll out the pastry and line a 9-in. (23-cm.) tart pan. Prick the surface with a fork and chill for 10 minutes in the freezer. Bake blind for 20 minutes. Remove from the oven and brush the base of the tart with lightly beaten egg.

Return to the oven for 10 to 15 minutes, until the edges are brown and the base of the crust is golden. Transfer to a wire rack and cool to room temperature. Assemble the tart as close to serving time as possible.

Whisk the cooled pastry cream and fill the tart shell, smoothing the top with a spatula. Carefully arrange the fruit in a decorative pattern over the pastry cream.

Warm the apricot jelly in a small saucepan over low heat. Add the water and stir until smooth. Using a pastry brush, glaze the fruit.

*Serves 6*

# brownie tart

see variations page 51

This tart elevates the brownie from snack food to a sophisticated dessert.

1/2 cup all-purpose flour
1/2 tsp. baking powder
1/2 tsp. salt
3 oz. unsweetened chocolate
1/3 cup unsalted butter

1 cup granulated sugar
2 large eggs, lightly beaten
1 tsp. vanilla extract
1/2 cup fresh raspberries

Preheat the oven to 350°F (175°C).

In a bowl combine the flour, baking powder, and salt. Set aside.

In a medium saucepan, melt the chocolate and butter over low heat, stirring to combine. Remove from the heat and stir in the sugar, eggs, and vanilla. Add the flour mixture and stir until just combined. Turn the mixture into a greased 9 1/2-in. (24-cm.) tart pan and bake for 20 minutes. Transfer to a wire rack to cool.

Garnish with fresh raspberries and serve with whipped cream.

*Serves 6–8*

# cherry pie with lattice top

see variations page 52

Nothing says summer like cherry pie!

| | |
|---|---|
| 1 recipe basic crust (page 18) | zest and juice of 1 lemon |
| 2/3 cup granulated sugar | 4 cups fresh or frozen, pitted |
| 3 tbsp. quick-cooking tapioca or cornstarch | sweet cherries |

Preheat the oven to 400°F (200°C). Mix the sugar, tapioca, and lemon zest and juice together. Pour the mixture over the cherries in a medium bowl and toss gently to coat evenly. Roll out half the quantity (one disc) of the pastry dough and line the bottom of a 9-in. (23-cm.) pie plate. Chill in the refrigerator while preparing the lattice.

Roll out the second disc of pastry dough. Using a pastry wheel or a sharp knife, cut into 1-in. (2.5-cm.) slices. Remove the bottom crust from the refrigerator and fill with the cherry mixture. Form the lattice top following the instructions on page 17.

Place the pie on a parchment paper–lined cookie sheet and bake for 20 minutes. Check the crust and if necessary cover the edges with aluminum foil to prevent overbrowning. Continue baking for 35 to 40 minutes, until the cherry filling bubbles and the crust is golden brown.

Transfer to a wire rack and cool for 1 hour. Serve warm or at room temperature.

*Serves 6–8*

# pecan pie

see variations page 53

This American classic has been popular since it first appeared in *The Fannie Farmer Cookbook*.

1/2 recipe basic crust (page 18)
2 tbsp. all-purpose flour
1 cup light brown sugar
3 large eggs
1 cup corn syrup

2 tbsp. unsalted butter, melted and cooled
2 tsp. vanilla extract
pinch of salt
2 cups pecan halves and pieces

Preheat the oven to 425°F (220°C). Roll out the pastry dough and line a 9-in. (23-cm.) pie plate. Crimp the edge decoratively. Chill in the refrigerator while making the filling.

Combine the flour and sugar in a large bowl. Whisk in the eggs, corn syrup, butter, vanilla, and salt. Mix in 1 cup of the pecans.

Remove the crust from the refrigerator and pour in the filling. Arrange or sprinkle the remaining pecans on top. Bake for 10 minutes. Lower the temperature to 325°F (160°C) and bake for another 45 minutes or until set.

Transfer to a wire rack and cool for an hour.

Serve with a dollop of whipped cream or vanilla ice cream.

*Serves 8*

# coconut cream pie

see variations page 54

This tropical-flavored custard cream pie is a long-standing classic in the Southern states.

1/2 recipe basic crust (page 18)
1/4 cup sweetened flaked coconut
4 large egg yolks
2/3 cup granulated sugar
1/4 cup cornstarch
1/4 tsp. salt
2 cups whole milk

1 cup unsweetened coconut milk
2 tbsp. unsalted butter, softened
1 tsp. vanilla extract
1 cup unsweetened flaked coconut
1 cup chilled whipping cream
2 tbsp. confectioners' sugar
1/8 tsp. coconut extract

Preheat the oven to 425°F (220°C). Roll out the pastry dough and line a 9-in. (23-cm.) pie plate. Prebake for 15 minutes. Transfer to a wire rack and lower the temperature to 375°F (190°C). Toast the sweetened coconut by spreading it on a parchment paper–lined cookie sheet and baking for 5 minutes. Reserve for topping. Using a fork, beat the egg yolks in a small bowl. Combine the sugar, cornstarch, and salt in a large saucepan. Slowly whisk in the milk and coconut milk over medium heat. Continue whisking until it reaches a boil. Cook for 1 minute, still whisking. Quickly transfer half the milk to the egg yolks. Whisk to combine, then return the egg and milk mixture to the saucepan. Return to boiling and cook for 1 minute, whisking continuously. Remove from the heat. Stir the butter, vanilla, and unsweetened coconut into the milk mixture. Pour into the piecrust. Cover with plastic wrap to prevent a skin from forming. Let cool, then refrigerate for 2 hours. Once set, beat the cream with the confectioners' sugar and coconut extract using an electric mixer until stiff. Remove the pie from the refrigerator. Top with the whipped cream and garnish with toasted coconut.

*Serves 6–8*

# french tarte tatin ☙

see variations page 55

This French classic features apples in a caramel sauce and a fluffy pastry baked in a skillet.

1/2 recipe basic crust (page 18)
    or frozen puff pastry, thawed
1 cup unsalted butter, softened

1 cup granulated sugar
4–5 medium apples, such as McIntosh

Preheat the oven to 400°F (200°C). In a small bowl cream the butter and sugar together. Spread the mixture evenly over the base and sides of a 9-in. (23-cm.) ovenproof skillet or flameproof dish. Peel and quarter the apples. Remove the cores to achieve a flat surface on the back of each apple quarter. Place the first quarter in the center of the skillet, flat side up. Form concentric circles with the remaining apple quarters. Fill in the gaps with smaller apple pieces, so that the skillet base is tightly packed with apples.

Cook over medium-high heat for 10 to 15 minutes, allowing the butter and sugar to melt and become a dark amber-colored caramel. Do not stir. The caramel should bubble up and cover the apple pieces. Cool to room temperature. Roll out the pastry dough or thawed puff pastry to a 10-in. (25-cm.) round. Cover the apples with the crust, tucking the excess pastry down the sides of the skillet. Bake for 25 to 30 minutes, until the crust is golden brown.

Transfer to a wire rack and cool for 30 minutes. Using oven mitts if the skillet is still hot, place a large dinner plate over the skillet and invert the tart onto the plate. Rearrange any misplaced apples. Serve warm with whipped cream.

*Serves 6*

# english bakewell tart

see variations page 56

This classic tart originated in England, where it is still enjoyed as a dessert or a teatime treat.

1/2 recipe basic sweet crust (page 20)
1 1/4 cups unsalted butter, softened
1 cup granulated sugar
2 1/4 cups finely ground blanched almonds

3 large eggs
1/3 cup strawberry jam
1/4 cup sliced blanched almonds or 1/2 cup
    blanched whole almonds

Preheat the oven to 350°F (175°C). Roll out the pastry dough and line a 10-in. (25-cm.) tart pan with a removable base. Prebake the crust for 15 minutes. Lower the temperature to 325°F (160°C).

In a medium bowl cream the butter and sugar with an electric mixer, then slowly add the ground almonds until well combined. Using a fork, beat the eggs and incorporate them into the almond mixture, then refrigerate for 20 minutes.

Using a spatula, spread the jam evenly over the base of the tart crust. Pour the chilled almond mixture over the layer of jam. Scatter the sliced almonds evenly over the top of the tart. Bake for 40 minutes or until the filling is firm and golden brown.

Transfer to a wire rack and cool for an hour. Serve with a dollop of whipped cream, crème fraiche, or clotted cream, if available.

*Serves 8*

# maple sugar tart  ✎

see variations page 57

This French-Canadian classic is traditionally prepared in early spring or "sugaring-off time." This pie is even better the following day, so try to prepare it in advance.

2/3 recipe basic crust (page 18)
2 1/4 cups maple sugar (sometimes sold as
    maple flakes), crumbled maple sugar candy,
    or light brown sugar
1 cup whipping cream
2/3 cup maple syrup, preferably "B" grade

1/4 cup unsalted butter, softened
1 large egg
3 tbsp. dry breadcrumbs
1/4 tsp. salt
1 tsp. vanilla extract

Preheat the oven to 350°F (175°C). Roll out the pastry dough slightly thicker than usual (1/4 in./5 mm. thick) and line a 10-in. (25-cm.) tart pan. Refrigerate for 20 minutes.

Whisk the sugar, cream, maple syrup, and butter in a saucepan over low heat. Cook for 10 minutes or until the sugar has dissolved, whisking regularly. Remove from the heat and cool for 30 minutes.

Using a fork, beat the egg and add to the maple mixture. Stir in the breadcrumbs, salt, and vanilla to blend. Pour into the chilled piecrust and bake for 40 to 45 minutes. The filling should be set and slightly raised in the center.

Transfer to a wire rack and cool completely. Serve with cream.

*Serves 8*

variations

# perfect apple pie

see base recipe page 31

### perfect apple-cranberry pie

Prepare the basic recipe, adding 1/2 cup sweetened, dried cranberries to the apple slices.

### perfect apple-pear pie

Prepare the basic recipe, replacing 3 of the apples with 3 ripe Bartlett or Anjou Pears.

### perfect apple pie with a streusel topping

Prepare the basic recipe, making 1/2 recipe basic crust and sprinkling streusel topping (page 28) over the apple mixture instead. If the crust is browning too quickly, cover the edges with aluminum foil.

### perfect apple pie in a cheddar crust

Prepare the basic recipe, replacing the basic crust recipe with the cheddar crust variation (page 19).

### perfect apple-ginger pie

Prepare the basic recipe, adding 1/4 cup minced candied ginger to the apple mixture.

variations

# lemon meringue pie

see base recipe page 33

### lemon meringue tart with a hazelnut crust
Prepare the basic recipe, replacing the basic crust with the hazelnut sweet crust variation (page 21), prebaked in an 11-in. (28-cm.) fluted tart pan.

### lemon-blueberry meringue pie
Prepare the basic recipe, folding 1 cup fresh blueberries into the cooled lemon curd before pouring the filling into the crust.

### lemon-ginger meringue pie
Prepare the basic recipe, adding 1/2 teaspoon grated fresh ginger to the lemon curd with the lemon zest. Garnish with 1/2 cup minced candied ginger.

### orange meringue pie
Prepare the basic recipe, replacing the lemon juice and zest with an equal quantity of orange juice and the zest of half an orange.

### lemon lattice meringue pie
Prepare the basic recipe, piping the meringue over the lemon curd filling with a lattice motif.

variations

# glazed fruit tart

see base recipe page 34

### glazed fruit tart with citrus-scented pastry cream
Prepare the basic recipe, replacing the basic pastry cream with the citrus-scented pastry cream variation (page 23).

### glazed tropical fruit tart
Prepare the basic recipe, using only sliced tropical fruit, such as mango, papaya, passion fruit, and kiwi.

### glazed fresh strawberry tart
Prepare the basic recipe, using only sliced strawberries on top.

### glazed fruit tart in vanilla sweet crust
Prepare the basic recipe, replacing the basic sweet crust with the vanilla sweet crust variation (page 21).

### glazed fruit tart in hazelnut sweet crust
Prepare the basic recipe, replacing the basic sweet crust with the hazelnut sweet crust variation (page 21).

variations

# brownie tart

see base recipe page 37

### polka-dot brownie tart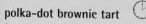
Prepare the basic recipe, arranging 1/4 cup white chocolate chips, pointy side down, in a pattern over the chocolate mixture once it has been spread in the tart pan.

### brownie tart with walnuts
Prepare the basic recipe, stirring in 1/4 cup chopped walnuts once the flour mixture has been combined.

### brownie tart with mandarin oranges
Prepare the basic recipe, arranging 1 cup drained canned mandarin slices in concentric circles over the top of the cooled tart.

### brownie tart with white chocolate drizzle
Prepare the basic recipe, drizzling 1/4 cup melted white chocolate in lines over the cooled tart.

### mocha brownie tart
Prepare the basic recipe, adding 1 teaspoon instant coffee to the chocolate mixture once removed from heat. Stir until the coffee has dissolved.

variations

# cherry pie with lattice top

see base recipe page 38

### cherry pie with coconut crumb topping
Prepare the basic recipe, making 1/2 recipe basic crust and replacing the
lattice top with crunchy coconut topping (page 29).

### cherry-almond pie with lattice top
Prepare the basic recipe, adding 1/4 teaspoon almond extract to the sugar
and tapioca mixture.

### sour cherry pie with lattice top
Prepare the basic recipe, replacing the sweet cherries with fresh sour
cherries. Increase the sugar to 1 cup and omit the lemon zest and juice.

### cherry-blueberry pie with lattice top
Prepare the basic recipe, reducing the amount of cherries to 2 cups,
and adding 2 cups of fresh blueberries. Add 1 teaspoon cinnamon
to the sugar mixture.

variations

# pecan pie

see base recipe page 41

### chocolate pecan pie
Prepare the basic recipe, adding 3 tablespoons unsweetened cocoa to the sugar.

### bourbon-spiked pecan pie
Prepare the basic recipe, adding 3 tablespoons bourbon to the filling.

### pecan–raisin pie
Prepare the basic recipe, adding 1/2 cup golden raisins to the filling once it has been whisked.

### mocha pecan pie with espresso cream
Prepare the basic recipe, adding 3 tablespoons unsweetened cocoa and 2 teaspoons instant espresso powder to the filling. Prepare the espresso cream by adding 1 teaspoon instant espresso powder and 2 tablespoons confectioners' sugar to 1 cup chilled whipping cream. Beat with an electric mixer until stiff.

### pecan pie with white chocolate drizzle
Prepare basic recipe, using a fork to drizzle 1/4 cup melted white chocolate over the top once the pie has cooled to room temperature.

# coconut cream pie

see base recipe page 42

### banana coconut cream pie
Prepare the basic recipe, lining the piecrust with slices from 2 large bananas. Proceed with assembly and garnish with more banana slices.

### coconut cream tartlets
Prepare the basic recipe, prebaking the piecrust in tartlet pans or a 12-cup muffin pan. Cover the filling with plastic wrap or parchment paper while still in the saucepan. Once the filling has cooled to room temperature, remove the tartlet crusts from their pans and assemble.

### coconut meringue pie
Prepare the basic recipe, omitting the whipped cream topping. Prepare the meringue as for lemon meringue pie (page 33). Top with meringue and brown carefully with a chef's blowtorch or in a preheated 375°F (190°C) oven for 12 to 15 minutes.

### coconut cream pie with crumb crust
Prepare the basic recipe, replacing the basic crust with the basic crumb crust (page 22).

### coconut cream pie with milk chocolate shavings
Prepare the basic recipe, garnishing with milk chocolate shavings.

# french tarte tatin

see base recipe page 43

### pear tarte tatin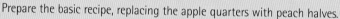
Prepare the basic recipe, replacing the apple quarters with pear quarters.
Trim the pointy ends off the pear pieces.

### peach tarte tatin
Prepare the basic recipe, replacing the apple quarters with peach halves.

### tarte tatin with calvados
Prepare the basic recipe, drizzling 2 tablespoons Calvados or other apple
liqueur over the apples before placing the crust on top.

### mini tartes tatin
Prepare the basic recipe, cutting the apples into 1/2-in. (1.5-cm.) pieces
instead of quarters. Put 2 tablespoons of the apple-caramel mixture
into each cup of a 12-cup muffin pan. Cut the basic crust or puff
pastry into 2 1/2-in. (6.5-cm.) circles and place one over each cup.
Bake for 25 to 30 minutes.

### tarte tatin with cheddar crust
Prepare the basic recipe, replacing the basic crust with the
cheddar crust variation (page 19).

variations

# english bakewell tart

see base recipe page 45

### bakewell tart with orange marmalade
Prepare the basic recipe, replacing the strawberry jam with an equal quantity of orange marmalade.

### bakewell tart with apricot jam
Prepare the basic recipe, replacing the strawberry jam with an equal quantity of apricot jam. Finely chop 1/4 cup dried apricots and scatter over the filling with the sliced almonds.

### bakewell tart with almond sweet crust
Prepare the basic recipe, replacing the basic sweet crust with the almond sweet crust variation (page 21).

### bakewell tart with raspberry jam
Prepare the basic recipe, replacing the strawberry jam with an equal quantity of raspberry jam. Garnish with fresh raspberries.

### bakewell tartlets
Prepare the basic recipe, prebaking the piecrust in individual tartlet pans or a 12-cup muffin pan. Proceed with pie assembly for each tartlet, and bake for 20 to 25 minutes.

variations

# maple sugar tart

see base recipe page 46

### espresso–maple sugar tart
Prepare the basic recipe, omitting the vanilla extract and adding 1 tablespoon coffee liqueur to the filling.

### orange–maple sugar tart
Prepare the basic recipe, using the citrus crust variation (page 19) in place of the basic crust. Omit the vanilla extract and add the zest and juice of one orange to the filling instead.

### pecan–maple sugar tart
Prepare the basic recipe, adding 1/2 cup pecan halves to the filling before pouring it into the piecrust.

### maple sugar tartlets
Prepare the basic recipe, lining individual tartlet pans or a 12-cup muffin pan with the piecrust. Refrigerate the tartlets while preparing the filling. Proceed with pie assembly for each tartlet. Bake for 20 to 25 minutes.

# fruit pies & tarts

It is hard to think of a fruit that doesn't work

splendidly in a pie. The possibilities are truly

endless in this chapter, which revisits tried and true

recipes and offers inspired variations.

# deep-dish peach pie

see variations page 76

If you love peaches, this is the pie for you. Be sure to have some good-quality vanilla ice cream to serve with it.

1 recipe basic crust (page 18)
1 cup light brown sugar
1/4 cup all-purpose flour
1/2 tsp. cinnamon

1/4 tsp. cardamom
1/4 tsp. nutmeg
10-12 large peaches, peeled, pitted, and sliced

Preheat the oven to 425°F (220°C).

Mix the sugar, flour, cinnamon, cardamom, and nutmeg together. Place the peaches in a large bowl, pour the mixture over them, and toss gently to coat evenly.

Roll out half the quantity (one disc) of the pastry dough and line a deep-dish 9-in. (23-cm.) pie plate. Pour the peaches into the pastry crust.

Roll out the second disc of pastry dough. Put the top crust on the pie, crimp the edges, and make 4 to 6 slits in the crust. Bake for 10 minutes. Lower the temperature to 350°F (175°C) and continue baking for an hour, or until the crust is golden brown.

Transfer to a wire rack and cool for 3 hours. Serve at room temperature.

*Serves 8*

# wild blueberry pie with cinnamon crust

see variations page 77

Take advantage of fresh wild blueberries abundant in late summer to make this delicious pie. You can also use frozen wild blueberries from your supermarket.

1 recipe cinnamon crust variation (page 19)
3/4 cup packed light brown sugar
1 tbsp. lemon juice
1/2 tsp. cinnamon

1/4 cup all-purpose flour
4 cups wild blueberries
1 tbsp. unsalted butter

Preheat the oven to 425°F (220°C). Mix the sugar, lemon juice, cinnamon, and flour together. Place the blueberries in a medium bowl, pour the mixture over them, and toss gently to coat evenly.

Roll out half the quantity (one disc) of the pastry dough and line a 9-in. (23-cm.) pie plate. Pour the blueberries into the crust and dot with butter.

Roll out the second disc of pastry dough. Put the top crust on the pie, crimp the edges, and make 4 to 6 slits in the crust. Bake for 30 minutes.

Lower the temperature to 350°F (175°C) and continue baking for 35 to 40 minutes, until the crust is golden brown. Transfer to a wire rack and cool for an hour. Serve the pie warm or at room temperature.

*Serves 6–8*

# pear & almond tart

see variations page 78

The combination of pears and almonds creates a luxurious, velvety texture in this classic French tart. This tart is delicious served with café au lait.

1 recipe almond sweet crust variation (page 21)
1 cup ground blanched almonds
2 tbsp. all-purpose flour
1/2 cup granulated sugar
6 tbsp. unsalted butter, softened

1 large egg
1/2 tsp. vanilla extract
14-oz. can pear halves in syrup
1 tbsp. confectioners' sugar (optional)
1/4 cup sliced almonds (optional)

Preheat the oven to 375°F (190°C). Roll out the pastry dough and line a 10-in. (25-cm.) tart pan. Chill in the freezer for 10 minutes. Bake blind for 15 minutes. Remove the parchment paper and weights, prick the bottom of the tart with a fork, and bake for another 10 minutes. Transfer to a wire rack to cool. Lower the temperature to 350°F (175°C).

In a medium bowl combine the ground almonds and flour. Mix in the sugar, then the butter. Add the egg and vanilla and stir until well combined. Refrigerate while preparing the pears. Place the pears on paper towels and pat dry. Cut across, but not through, each pear half to create thin, fanlike slices. Spread the chilled almond filling over the base of the tart crust. Arrange the pear halves over the filling, fanning out the slices so the narrow ends meet at the center of the tart. Bake for 45 minutes, until the almond filling is puffed and golden brown. Transfer to a wire rack to cool.

Dust with confectioners' sugar and garnish with almond slices, if desired.

*Serves 6*

# strawberry, rhubarb & orange pie

see variations page 79

This early summer classic gets an update with a hint of orange.

1 recipe basic crust (page 18)
1 cup granulated sugar
zest of 1 orange
2 tbsp. orange juice
1/2 tsp. cinnamon

pinch of nutmeg
1/4 cup cornstarch
3 cups rhubarb, cut to 1/2-in. (1.5-cm.) lengths
2 cups strawberries, hulled and halved

Preheat the oven to 425°F (220°C). Mix the sugar, orange zest and juice, cinnamon, nutmeg, and cornstarch together. Place the rhubarb and strawberries in a large bowl, pour the mixture over them, and toss gently to coat the fruit evenly.

Roll out half the quantity (one disc) of the pastry dough and line a 9-in. (23-cm.) pie plate. Pour the fruit mixture into the piecrust.

Roll out the second disc of pastry dough. Put the top crust on the pie, crimp the edges, and make 4 to 6 slits in the crust. Bake for 10 minutes.

Lower the temperature to 350°F (175°C) and continue baking for 35 to 40 minutes, until the crust is golden brown. Transfer to a wire rack and cool completely.

*Serves 6*

# banana & toffee "banoffee" pie

see variations page 80

This pie is said to have been created in an English pub called the Hungry Monk.

1/2 recipe basic crust (page 18)
2 firm, ripe bananas
1 tbsp. lemon juice
2 1/3 cups dulce de leche, store-bought
    or homemade

1 cup whipping cream
2 tbsp. granulated sugar
1/2 tsp. cinnamon

Preheat the oven to 425°F (220°C). Roll out the pastry dough and line a 9-in. (23-cm.) pie plate.

Prick the surface with a fork and bake for 15 minutes. Transfer to a wire rack to cool.

Slice the bananas and toss in a medium bowl with the lemon juice. Spread the dulce de leche evenly over the base of the cooled piecrust.

Arrange the sliced bananas evenly on top. Using an electric mixer, beat the cream with the sugar until stiff. Spoon the cream over the banana layer. Dust with cinnamon.

Chill until ready to serve. Refrigerate any remaining pie for up to 3 days.

*Serves 6–8*

# lemon tart

see variations page 81

This easy yet elegant tart is just the thing for a delightful afternoon tea in the garden.

1 recipe basic sweet crust (page 20)
1 large egg, lightly beaten
1/2 cup fresh lemon juice
6 large egg yolks
1 cup granulated sugar

1/2 cup (8 tbsp.) unsalted butter
zest of 3 lemons
1 tbsp. confectioners' sugar
1 lemon, sliced

Preheat the oven to 400°F (200°C). Roll out the pastry dough and line a 9-in. (23-cm.) pan. Prick the surface with a fork and chill for 10 minutes in the freezer. Bake blind for 20 minutes. Remove from the oven and brush the base of the tart with lightly beaten egg. Return to the oven for 10 to 15 minutes, until the base of the crust is golden. Transfer to a wire rack to cool. In a medium bowl, whisk the lemon juice, egg yolks, and sugar until smooth. Transfer the mixture to a heavy-based saucepan and cook over medium heat until the mixture begins to thicken, about 10 minutes. Take care not to let the mixture boil. When the curd is thick enough to coat a wooden spoon, reduce the heat to low and continue cooking for 10 more minutes. Remove from the heat and stir in the butter, until melted. Strain the curd through a fine sieve into a medium bowl and stir in the lemon zest. Pour the lukewarm curd into the tart shell. For ease of slicing, chill for at least 1 hour in the refrigerator. Dust with confectioners' sugar and garnish with lemon slices. Refrigerate any remaining pie for up to 3 days.

**QUICK & EASY SHORTCUT:** Replace the lemon filling with 2 cups store-bought lemon curd.

*Serves 6–8*

# pineapple & mango pie

see variations page 82

Make this tropical-flavored pie on a cold day and watch your winter blues disappear.

1 recipe basic crust (see page 18)
3 cups fresh pineapple, cut into 1/2-in.
  (1.5-cm.) chunks
1 cup fresh mango, cut into 1/2-in.
  (1.5-cm.) chunks

2/3 cup granulated sugar
1/4 cup all-purpose flour
pinch of salt
3 large eggs, lightly beaten
1/4 cup unsalted butter, melted and cooled

Preheat the oven to 425°F (220°C).

Roll out half the quantity (one disc) of pastry dough and line a 9-in. (23-cm.) pie plate.

Place the pineapple and mango chunks over the base of the piecrust. Combine the sugar, flour, and salt in a medium bowl. Stir in the eggs and melted butter until well combined. Pour the sugar and egg mixture over the fruit.

Roll out the second disc of pastry dough. Put the top crust on the pie, crimp the edges, and make 4 to 6 slits in the crust. Bake for 10 minutes.

Lower the temperature to 325°F (160°C) and continue baking for 1 hour, until the crust is golden brown.

*Serves 6–8*

# rustic pear &
# blackberry galette

see variations page 83

This free-form pie is baked on a cookie sheet lined with parchment paper, so cleanup is minimal and enjoyment is complete.

1/2 recipe basic crust (page 18)
2 tbsp. all-purpose flour
2 tbsp. light brown sugar
4 firm, ripe pears, Bosc or Anjou variety,
    sliced thinly

1/2 cup fresh blackberries
3 tbsp. granulated sugar
1/2 tsp. cinnamon
1 tbsp. confectioners' sugar

Preheat the oven to 375°F (190°C). Roll out the pastry dough into a 13-in. (33-cm.) round. Transfer to a cookie sheet lined with parchment paper, or roll out directly onto the parchment paper and slide the paper onto the cookie sheet.

Mix the flour and the brown sugar. Spread the mixture evenly over the pastry round, leaving a 2-in. (5-cm.) border. Arrange the pear slices over the sugar mixture. Dot the pears with blackberries. Mix the granulated sugar with the cinnamon and sprinkle over the fruit. Fold the edge of the crust over the pears, making any necessary pleats. Cover the galette loosely with foil and bake for 40 minutes. Uncover and bake for 5 minutes, or until the fruit is bubbling and tender and the crust is golden brown. Transfer to a wire rack and sprinkle with confectioners' sugar. Serve the galette warm with fresh cream.

*Serves 6*

# raspberry-almond jalousie

see variations page 84

The jalousie takes its name from a type of French window shutter made with horizontal slats. Using store-bought puff pastry and raspberry jam makes this sophisticated pastry easy to make at home.

1/2 package frozen puff pastry, thawed
2 cups good-quality raspberry jam
1/4 cup sliced almonds,
  toasted and roughly chopped

1 large egg, beaten (for glaze)
2 tbsp. sugar

Preheat the oven to 400°F (200°C). Line a cookie sheet with parchment paper. On a lightly floured surface, roll out the puff pastry to form a 16 x 12-in. (40 x 30-cm.) rectangle. Using a sharp knife, cut the rectangle in half, making two 16 x 6-in. (40 x 15-cm.) rectangles. Place the first rectangle on the lined cookie sheet, and cover the pastry with raspberry jam, leaving a 1-in. (2.5-cm.) border on all sides. Sprinkle the chopped almonds over the jam. Using a pastry brush, glaze the border with beaten egg. Place the second rectangle on top of the first, pressing down the edges to seal. Again, glaze a 1-in. (2.5-cm.) border with beaten egg, and fold over to create a 1/2-in. (1.5-cm.) trim. Crimp decoratively.

Glaze the pastry with beaten egg and dust with sugar. Using a sharp knife, make 2-in. (5-cm.) slits along the top layer of the pastry at 1-in. (2.5-cm.) intervals, leaving a 1-in. (2.5-cm.) border between the slits and trim. Bake for 25 minutes, until the pastry is golden brown.

Transfer to a wire rack and cool. Serve with vanilla ice cream.

*Serves 4–6*

# glazed kiwi & lime tart with pistachio crust

see variations page 85

The combination of kiwi and lime is amazingly refreshing. Perfect barbeque fare.

1 cup finely ground pistachio nuts
1 cup graham cracker crumbs
1/4 cup granulated sugar
1 tbsp. lime zest
6 tbsp. unsalted butter, melted and cooled
2 large egg yolks
14-oz. can condensed milk

1/2 cup fresh lime juice
5 kiwis, peeled and sliced into thin rounds
1 tbsp. fresh lime juice
1 tbsp. water
1 tbsp. granulated sugar
1/2 tsp. cornstarch

Preheat the oven to 350°F (175°C). Grease a 9-in. (23-cm.) fluted tart pan. Combine the pistachios, graham cracker crumbs, sugar, and lime zest in a food processor. Blend in the butter until the mixture is moistened. Press the crust into the tart pan. Bake for 10 minutes. Transfer to a wire rack and cool. Beat the egg yolks, condensed milk, and 1/2 cup of lime juice until well combined. Pour into the cooled crust, and even the surface with a spatula. Bake for 15 minutes. Transfer to a wire rack. Arrange the kiwi slices on top of the filling — slightly overlapping, in concentric circles.

Mix the tablespoon of lime juice, water, sugar, and cornstarch in a medium saucepan. Over medium heat bring the glaze to a boil, stirring constantly until it thickens. Remove from the heat. Using a pastry brush, cover the kiwis with the glaze. Refrigerate until ready to serve, for at least 1 hour.

*Serves 6*

variations

# deep-dish peach pie

see base recipe page 59

### deep-dish vanilla-peach pie
Prepare the basic recipe, adding 1 teaspoon vanilla extract to the sugar mixture.

### deep-dish peach pie with lattice top
Prepare the basic recipe. Using a sharp knife or pastry wheel, cut the top crust into strips and arrange them in a lattice form (page 17).

### deep-dish peach & blackberry pie
Prepare the basic recipe, reducing the number of peaches to 8 and adding 2 cups of blackberries to the fruit mixture.

### deep-dish nectarine pie
Prepare the basic recipe, replacing the peaches with fresh nectarines.

### deep-dish peach pie with streusel topping
Prepare the basic recipe, making 1/2 the basic crust recipe. Top with streusel topping (page 28).

variations

# wild blueberry pie with cinnamon crust

see base recipe page 61

### wild blueberry pie with basic crust
Prepare the basic recipe, replacing the cinnamon crust with the basic crust.

### wild blueberry pie with lattice crust
Prepare the basic recipe, forming a lattice top with the second disc (half the quantity) of the cinnamon pastry. Follow the instructions for a lattice top on page 17.

### wild blueberry pie with cardamom
Prepare the basic recipe, replacing the 1/2 teaspoon cinnamon in the filling with 1/4 teaspoon ground cardamom.

### wild blueberry-lemon pie
Prepare the basic recipe, replacing the cinnamon crust with the citrus crust variation (page 19). Add the zest of 1 lemon to the filling.

### wild blueberry-raspberry pie
Prepare the basic recipe, reducing the amount of wild blueberries to 2 cups and adding 2 cups of fresh raspberries to the filling.

variations

# pear & almond tart

see base recipe page 62

### peach & almond tart
Prepare the basic recipe, replacing the pear halves with canned peach halves.

### plum & almond tart
Prepare the basic recipe, replacing the pear halves with fresh red plums, pitted and sliced. Arrange in overlapping concentric circles over the filling.

### fig & almond tart
Prepare the basic recipe, replacing the pears with 4 to 5 ripe figs. Cut the figs in half, then slice across and fan out in the same manner as the pear slices.

### banana almond tart
Prepare the basic recipe, replacing the pears with thin slices from 4 to 5 firm, ripe bananas. Toss the banana slices in a medium bowl with 1 tablespoon lemon juice. Arrange the slices over the almond filling, slightly overlapping.

### glazed pear & almond tart
Prepare the basic recipe, reserving 3/4 cup syrup from the canned pears. In a saucepan, combine the syrup and 1/2 teaspoon vanilla extract. Reduce the syrup to 1/4 cup. Whisk in 1 teaspoon cornstarch and cook until the cornstarch has dissolved and the mixture thickens. Using a pastry brush, glaze the cooled tart.

variations

# strawberry, rhubarb & orange pie

see base recipe page 64

### strawberry-rhubarb pie
Prepare the basic recipe, omitting the orange juice and zest.

### strawberry, rhubarb & ginger pie
Prepare the basic recipe, omitting the orange juice and zest and adding
1/2 cup minced candied ginger.

### strawberry-rhubarb pie with streusel topping
Prepare the basic recipe making 1/2 basic crust recipe. Instead of a top
crust, sprinkle the filling with streusel topping (page 28).

### strawberry, rhubarb & orange pie in a citrus crust
Prepare the basic recipe, replacing the basic crust with the citrus
crust variation (page 19).

variations

# banana & toffee "banoffee" pie

see base recipe page 65

### apple toffee pie
Prepare the basic recipe, replacing the banana slices with an equal quantity of apple slices.

### strawberry toffee pie
Prepare the basic recipe, replacing the banana slices with an equal quantity of strawberry slices.

### pineapple toffee pie
Prepare the basic recipe, replacing the banana slices with an equal quantity of pineapple slices.

### peach toffee pie
Prepare the basic recipe, replacing the banana slices with an equal quantity of peach slices.

### banana toffee pie with bailey's scented whipped cream
Prepare the basic recipe, adding 1 tablespoon Bailey's Irish Cream to the whipped cream and confectioners' sugar.

variations

# lemon tart

see base recipe page 67

### blood orange tart
Prepare the basic recipe, replacing the lemon juice with an equal quantity of
blood orange juice. Replace the lemon zest with zest from 1/2 blood orange.

### caramelized lemon tart
Prepare the basic recipe. Sprinkle 1 tablespoon granulated sugar over the top
of the cooled tart. Place under a preheated broiler, until the sugar caramelizes.

### pink grapefruit tart
Prepare the basic recipe, replacing the lemon juice with an equal quantity
of pink grapefruit juice. Replace the lemon zest with zest from 1/4 pink
grapefruit. Garnish with pink grapefruit slices.

### lemon tart with meringue lattice top
Prepare the basic recipe, piping four stripes of meringue across the tart, then
four more stripes across the first four to form a lattice top. Place the tart
under a preheated broiler until the meringue begins to brown.

### lemon tart in hazelnut crust
Prepare the basic recipe, replacing the basic sweet crust with the hazelnut
sweet crust variation (page 21).

variations

# pineapple & mango pie

see base recipe page 68

### pineapple & papaya pie
Prepare the basic recipe, replacing the mango chunks with an equal quantity of papaya chunks.

### pineapple & mango pie with crunchy coconut topping
Prepare the basic recipe, making 1/2 the basic crust recipe. Combine 1/2 cup sweetened flaked coconut and 1/3 cup chopped macadamia nuts, pecans, or walnuts. Spread the coconut topping over the filling, pressing lightly into the filling. Bake in a preheated 325°F (160°C) oven for 1 hour 15 minutes.

### spiked pineapple & mango pie
Prepare the basic recipe, adding 2 tablespoons dark rum to the sugar and egg mixture.

### pineapple & mango pie in cinnamon crust
Prepare the basic recipe, replacing the basic crust with the cinnamon crust variation (page 19).

# rustic pear & blackberry galette

see base recipe page 71

### rustic pear & blackberry galette with cornmeal crust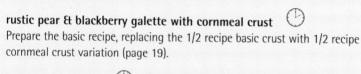
Prepare the basic recipe, replacing the 1/2 recipe basic crust with 1/2 recipe cornmeal crust variation (page 19).

### rustic plum galette
Prepare the basic recipe, replacing the fruit with 5 large ripe plums, red or black, sliced thinly.

### rustic apple galette
Prepare the basic recipe, replacing the fruit with 4 medium sliced apples.

### rustic pear & honey galette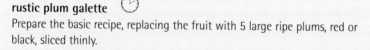
Prepare the basic recipe, omitting the sugar and flour mixture. Toss the pear slices in 2 tablespoons honey and 1 tablespoon lemon juice. Sprinkle with chopped fresh thyme.

### rustic peach galette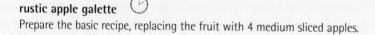
Prepare the basic recipe, replacing the plums with 4 large sliced peaches.

variations

# raspberry-almond jalousie

see base recipe page 72

### apple-raspberry jalousie

Prepare the basic recipe, spreading a layer of apple slices on the first rectangle of puff pastry. Dot the apple slices with 1 tablespoon unsalted butter, then sprinkle with 2 tablespoons brown sugar and 1/4 teaspoon cinnamon. Spread raspberry jam over the apples and proceed.

### rhubarb-raspberry jalousie

Prepare the basic recipe. Melt 2 tablespoons unsalted butter in a saucepan. Add 4 cups sliced rhubarb and 1/4 cup granulated sugar to the butter and cook until the rhubarb becomes soft and mushy, about 10 minutes. Reduce the raspberry jam to 1 cup. Add jam to the rhubarb mixture, cool, and proceed.

### gooseberry jalousie

Prepare the basic recipe, replacing the raspberry jam with gooseberry jam.

### orange jalousie

Prepare the basic recipe, replacing the raspberry jam with marmalade.

### chocolate-hazelnut jalousie

Prepare the basic recipe, replacing the jam with chocolate-hazelnut spread. Substitute 1/4 cup roughly chopped, toasted hazelnuts for the almonds.

variations

# glazed kiwi & lime tart with pistachio crust

see base recipe page 75

### glazed strawberry & lime tart with pistachio crust
Prepare the basic recipe, replacing the sliced kiwis with 2 cups sliced strawberries. Proceed with glazing.

### glazed raspberry & lime tart with pistachio crust
Prepare the basic recipe, replacing the sliced kiwis with 2 cups fresh raspberries. Proceed with glazing.

### glazed blueberry, kiwi & lime tart with pistachio crust
Prepare the basic recipe, arranging a handful of fresh blueberries over the kiwi slices. Proceed with glazing.

### glazed mango & lime tart with pistachio crust
Prepare the basic recipe, replacing the kiwi slices with 2 cups sliced mango. Proceed with glazing.

# cream, custard & chiffon pies

These luscious pies and tarts are a decadent way to

end a meal or simply indulge a late-night craving.

# peach cloud pie

see variations page 104

Using the ripest fruit at the height of peach season will guarantee the success of this pie.

1/2 recipe basic crust (page 18)
4 large peaches
1 1/2 tbsp. fresh lemon juice
1/2 cup granulated sugar

1 envelope unflavored gelatin
1/4 cup water
3 large egg whites
2/3 cup whipping cream

Preheat the oven to 425°F (220°C). Roll out the crust and line a 9-in. (23-cm.) pie plate. Crimp the edge decoratively and prick the bottom and sides with a fork. Bake blind for 15 minutes. Remove the paper and weights and bake for 10 minutes more, until the crust is golden brown. Transfer to a wire rack and cool. Peel and quarter the peaches. Blend with the lemon juice and 1/4 cup of the sugar in a food processor until smooth. Sprinkle the gelatin over the water in a saucepan. Set aside while you fill a large bowl with ice and cold water. Add the peach purée to the gelatin and cook for 3 to 4 minutes, stirring until the gelatin has dissolved. Pour the peach mixture into a metal bowl and set the bowl in the ice bath. Chill, stirring occasionally, for 10 to 15 minutes, until the mixture begins to thicken.

Whisk the egg whites with an electric mixer. When they become foamy, begin adding the remaining 1/4 cup sugar, a tablespoon at a time. Continue whisking until stiff. In another bowl, beat the whipping cream on medium-high speed. Gently fold the cream into the peach mixture. Fold the egg whites into the peach and cream mixture, 1/3 cup at a time, until well combined. Pour the filling into the cooled piecrust and refrigerate for 3 hours, or until the the filling has set. Refrigerate any remaining pie for up to 3 days.

*Serves 6–8*

# blueberry-yogurt cream pie

see variations page 105

Yogurt is the twist in this blueberry pie that will keep you coming back for more.

1 recipe basic crumb crust (page 22)
1 envelope unflavored gelatin
3 tbsp. water
1 cup whipping cream

2 cups whole-milk vanilla yogurt
1/4 cup granulated sugar
2 cups fresh blueberries

Preheat the oven to 350°F (175°C). Line a 9-in. (23-cm.) pie plate with the crumb crust and bake for 15 minutes. Transfer to a wire rack and leave to cool.

In a small saucepan sprinkle the gelatin over the water. Set aside for a few minutes while you fill a large bowl with ice and cold water. Then cook the gelatin for 3 to 4 minutes, stirring continuously until it has dissolved. Pour the gelatin mixture into a metal bowl filled with 1/4 cup of the whipping cream.

In a separate bowl, stir the yogurt and sugar together. Gently whisk the yogurt mixture into the metal bowl with the gelatin mixture, then set the bowl in the ice bath. Chill, stirring occasionally, for 10 to 15 minutes, until the mixture begins to thicken. Using an electric mixer, beat the remaining cream into stiff peaks. Gently fold the cream and 1 3/4 cups of the blueberries into the chilled yogurt and gelatin mixture. Pour the mixture into the cooled piecrust and place the remaining 1/4 cup blueberries over the filling.

Refrigerate for 30 minutes, or until set.

*Serves 6–8*

# chocolate cream tart

see variations page 106

Make this for your favorite chocoholics. It is a dessert for children and adults alike.

1 recipe chocolate wafer crumb crust variation
  (page 22)
4 large egg yolks
2/3 cup granulated sugar
1/4 cup cornstarch
1/4 tsp. salt
3 cups whole milk

4 oz. semisweet chocolate, melted and cooled
3 oz. unsweetened chocolate, melted and cooled
2 tbsp. unsalted butter, softened
1 tsp. vanilla extract
1 cup whipping cream, chilled
2 tbsp. confectioners' sugar
1 tbsp. Dutch-process unsweetened cocoa

Preheat the oven to 350°F (175°C). Line a 9-in. (23-cm.) fluted tart pan with the chocolate wafer crumb crust. Bake for 15 minutes. Using a fork, beat the egg yolks in a small bowl. Combine the sugar, cornstarch, and salt in a large saucepan. Slowly whisk in the milk over medium heat. Continue whisking until the mixture reaches a boil. Cook for 1 minute, still whisking. Quickly transfer half the milk mixture to the egg yolks. Whisk to combine, then return the egg yolk and milk mixture to the saucepan. Return to a boil and cook for 1 minute, continuously whisking. Remove from heat. Stir the melted chocolates, butter, and vanilla into the milk mixture. Cover with plastic wrap or parchment paper to prevent a skin from forming. Let cool to room temperature before refrigerating for 2 hours to set. Fill the baked piecrust with the chocolate filling. Chill for 6 hours. Using an electric mixer, beat the cream with the confectioners' sugar until stiff. Remove the pie from the refrigerator. Top the filling with the cream and dust with cocoa. Refrigerate any remaining pie after serving.

**QUICK & EASY SHORTCUT:** Replace the filling with 2 cups store-bought chocolate pudding.

*Serves 6–8*

# pink grapefruit custard tart

see variations page 107

The contrasting natures of the tart pink grapefruit and smooth egg custard prove that opposites attract in this tantalizing dessert.

1 recipe basic sweet crust (page 20)
2/3 cup granulated sugar
4 large eggs
1/2 tsp. almond extract (optional)

3/4 cup whipping cream
3/4 cup fresh pink grapefruit juice
2 large pink grapefruit
1 tbsp. confectioners' sugar

Preheat the oven to 375°F (190°C). Roll out the pastry dough and transfer to a 10-in. (25-cm.) tart pan. Prick the surface with a fork and prebake for 15 minutes. Transfer to a wire rack to cool.

Whisk the sugar, eggs, and almond extract (if using) together. Pour the cream into the mixture, whisking gently. Continue whisking while adding the fresh grapefruit juice. Strain the custard through a fine sieve to remove any lumps. Pour the custard into the cooled tart crust and bake for 40 minutes, until the center of the tart is set and the crust is golden brown. Transfer to a wire rack to cool.

Preheat a broiler. Peel the grapefruit and carefully separate the segments from the pith and membrane. Place the segments on an aluminum foil–lined cookie sheet and place under the broiler for no more than 4 minutes, flipping the fruit after 2 minutes. Dust the tart crust with confectioners' sugar and serve with the roasted grapefruit segments.

*Serves 8*

# lemon mousse pie

see variations page 108

This light and refreshing dessert gets a little extra zing from the gingersnap crust!

1 recipe gingersnap crumb crust variation
   (page 22)
3/4 cup fresh lemon juice
zest of 1 lemon
3/4 cup granulated sugar
3 large egg yolks

pinch of salt
1 envelope unflavored gelatin
1/4 cup water
1 cup whipping cream
1/3 cup confectioners' sugar
zest of 1 lemon to decorate

Preheat the oven to 350°F (175°C). Press the gingersnap crumb crust into a 9-in. (23-cm.) pie plate. Bake for 15 minutes. Transfer to a wire rack and cool to room temperature.

Blend the lemon juice, zest, sugar, egg yolks, and salt in a medium saucepan. Cook over medium heat until the mixture thickens slightly — not as much as lemon curd. Sprinkle the gelatin over the water in a large saucepan. Set aside for a few minutes while you fill a large bowl with ice and cold water. Add the lemon mixture to the gelatin and cook over medium-low heat for 3 to 4 minutes, stirring continuously until the gelatin has dissolved. Pour the mixture into a metal bowl and set the bowl in the ice bath. Chill, stirring occasionally, for 10 to 15 minutes, until it begins to thicken. Beat the cream using an electric mixer, adding 1 tablespoon confectioners' sugar at a time. Gently fold the cream into the lemon mixture, 1/3 cup at a time, until well combined. Pour the filling into the piecrust and refrigerate for 3 hours, or until the filling has set. Sprinkle with the lemon zest and serve with a dollop of whipped cream. Refrigerate any remaining pie for up to 3 days.

*Serves 6–8*

# banana cream pie

see variations page 109

The pairing of bananas and cream is always a crowd pleaser!

1 recipe basic crumb crust (page 22)
3 large egg yolks
1/2 cup granulated sugar
1/3 cup cornstarch
1/4 tsp. salt
1 1/2 cups whole milk
1 1/2 cups whipping cream
2 tbsp. unsalted butter, softened

2 tsp. vanilla extract
4 firm, ripe bananas
1 tbsp. lemon juice
1 cup whipping cream, chilled
2 tbsp. confectioners' sugar
1 banana, sliced, to decorate
cinnamon, to dust

Preheat the oven to 350°F (175°C). Line a 9-in. (23-cm.) pie plate with the crust. Bake for 15 minutes. Transfer to a wire rack to cool. Using a fork, beat the egg yolks in a small bowl. Combine the sugar, cornstarch, and salt in a saucepan. Slowly whisk in the milk, 1 1/2 cups whipping cream, and vanilla over medium heat, until the mixture reaches a boil. Cook for 1 minute, still whisking. Quickly transfer half the milk mixture to the egg yolks. Whisk to combine; return the egg and milk mixture to the saucepan. Return to a boil and cook until thickened, about 6 minutes, continuously whisking. Remove from heat and whisk in the butter until melted. Cover with plastic wrap and let cool before refrigerating for 2 hours. Cut the bananas into 1/2-in. (1.5-cm.) slices and toss gently in a bowl with the lemon juice. Fill the piecrust with 1 cup of filling. Arrange a layer of banana slices. Repeat the layers twice more. Cover loosely with plastic wrap and chill for 6 hours. Beat the chilled cream and confectioners' sugar with an electric mixer until stiff. Remove the pie from the refrigerator. Top the filling with the cream and banana slices, and dust with cinnamon. Refrigerate any remaining pie.

*Serves 6–8*

# maple custard tart

see variations page 110

The subtle flavors of maple and cinnamon in this simple and elegant tart make this a perfect brunch offering.

1 recipe basic sweet crust (page 20)
4 large eggs
1 cup plain yogurt

3/4 cup maple syrup
1/2 tsp. cinnamon
pinch of salt

Preheat the oven to 375°F (190°C). Place a parchment paper-lined cookie sheet in the oven.

Roll out the pastry dough and transfer to an 11-in. (28-cm.) tart pan.

Beat the eggs, yogurt, maple syrup, cinnamon, and salt with an electric mixer on high until well combined. Remove the cookie sheet from the oven. Place the tart tin on the hot sheet and pour the filling into the tart crust. Bake for 45 minutes, or until the filling is golden brown and puffed up.

Transfer to a wire rack and cool. Refrigerate any remaining pie for up to 3 days.

*Serves 8*

# bavarian apple-almond torte

see variations page 111

With a shortbreadlike crust, cheesecakelike filling, and apple-almond topping, this classic torte truly has something to offer everybody.

1 recipe confectioners' sugar sweet crust
    variation (page 21)
1 cup cream cheese, softened
1/4 cup confectioners' sugar
1 large egg
1 tsp. vanilla extract

1/3 cup granulated sugar
1/2 tsp. cinnamon
pinch of nutmeg
3-4 cooking apples, such as McIntosh
    or Golden Delicious, sliced thinly
1/4 cup sliced almonds

Preheat the oven to 375°F (190°C). Roll out the pastry dough and transfer to a 10-in. (25-cm.) tart pan. Bake blind for 15 minutes. Transfer to a wire rack to cool. Lower the temperature to 350°F (175°C).

To prepare the filling, beat the cream cheese, confectioners' sugar, egg, and vanilla with an electric mixer on medium until smooth. Pour into the cooled tart crust and spread with a spatula to make an even surface.

To prepare the topping, mix the sugar, cinnamon, and nutmeg in a large bowl. Add the apple slices and toss to coat evenly. Arrange the apples over the cream cheese filling. Top with sliced almonds. Bake for 1 1/2 hours, or until the crust is golden brown and the apples are softened. Transfer to a wire rack and cool for 1 hour. Refrigerate any remaining pie for up to 3 days.

*Serves 6*

# raspberry chiffon pavlova

see variations page 112

The pavlova originated in Australia, where a chef created the dessert for the famous ballerina of the same name.

3 large egg whites
1/4 tsp. cream of tartar
1/2 tsp. vanilla extract
1/3 cup superfine sugar
3 cups frozen raspberries, thawed
1 tsp. lemon juice
1/3 cup granulated sugar
1 envelope unflavored gelatin

1/4 cup water
3 large egg whites
1/4 cup superfine sugar
2/3 cup whipping cream
1 cup fresh raspberries
1 tbsp. confectioners' sugar
a few fresh mint leaves (optional)

Preheat the oven to 275°F (135°C). Line a cookie sheet with parchment paper and trace a 9-in. (23-cm.) circle on it. Using an electric mixer, beat the egg whites and cream of tartar on high speed. When the egg whites become foamy add the vanilla, then begin beating in the superfine sugar, 1 tablespoon at a time. Continue beating until the meringue is stiff and glossy. Do not underbeat the meringue, or it will not set properly. Spoon the meringue onto the cookie sheet, spreading it over the parchment circle and building up the sides. Bake for 1 1/2 hours. Turn off the oven, but leave the meringue to sit in it for at least 1 hour (or overnight). To make the filling, blend the thawed raspberries with the lemon juice and the granulated sugar in the food processor until smooth. Strain the raspberry purée through a fine sieve. Discard the seeds. Sprinkle the gelatin over the water in a large saucepan. Set aside for a few minutes while you prepare an ice bath by filling a large bowl with ice and

*Serves 6–8*

cold water. Transfer the raspberry purée to the saucepan with the gelatin and cook over medium-low heat for 3 to 4 minutes, stirring continuously, until the gelatin has dissolved. Pour the raspberry and gelatin mixture into a metal bowl and set the bowl in the ice bath. Chill, stirring occasionally, for 10 to 15 minutes, until the mixture begins to thicken. Beat the remaining egg whites with an electric mixer. When they become foamy, begin adding 1/4 cup superfine sugar, 1 tablespoon at a time. Continue whisking until stiff. In another bowl, beat the cream on medium-high speed. Gently fold the whipped cream into the raspberry mixture. Fold the meringue into the raspberry and cream mixture, 1/3 cup at a time, until well combined. Spoon the filling into the meringue shell and refrigerate for 3 hours, or until set. Toss the fresh raspberries in confectioners' sugar and sprinkle over the filling just before serving. Garnish with a few fresh mint leaves if desired. Refrigerate any remaining pie for up to 3 days.

# butterscotch chiffon pie

see variations page 113

This decadent pie will melt in your mouth.

1/2 recipe basic crust (page 18)
1 egg, lightly beaten
2 tbsp. water
3 tbsp. light corn syrup
3/4 cup granulated sugar

1/4 cup unsalted butter
pinch of salt
1 tsp. apple cider vinegar
1/3 cup whipping cream
1 tsp. vanilla extract

2 tsp. unflavored gelatin
2 tbsp. water
3 large egg whites
1 tbsp. granulated sugar
1 cup whipping cream

Preheat the oven to 425°F (220°C). Roll out the pastry dough and line a 9-in. (23-cm.) pie plate. Crimp the edge and prick the bottom and sides with a fork. Brush the edge with egg and bake for 15 minutes. Transfer to a wire rack to cool. Combine the water, corn syrup, and sugar together in a heavy-based saucepan. Stir over low heat until the sugar has dissolved. Stop stirring, and bring to a boil. Boil for 10 minutes, occasionally swirling the liquid around the saucepan. When the mixture turns to dark amber, remove from heat. Cool for a few minutes, then add the butter, salt, and vinegar. Swirl to melt the butter. Add 1/3 cup whipping cream, return to the heat, and simmer for 1 minute, stirring gently. Remove from the heat. Sprinkle the gelatin over 2 tablespoons water in a small saucepan. Cook over medium-low heat for 3 to 4 minutes, stirring occasionally, until the gelatin has dissolved. Add the gelatin mixture to the butterscotch and transfer to a large bowl. Whisk the egg whites with an electric mixer. When they become foamy, add 1 tablespoon sugar. Continue beating until stiff. In another bowl, beat 1 cup cream on medium-high speed. Gently fold the whipped cream into the butterscotch mixture. Fold the egg whites into the butterscotch and cream mixture, 1/3 cup at a time, until well combined. Pour the filling into the cooled piecrust and refrigerate for 3 hours, or until the filling has set. Refrigerate any remaining pie for up to 3 days.

*Serves 6–8*

# peach cloud pie

see base recipe page 87

### nectarine cloud pie
Prepare the basic recipe, replacing the peaches with an equal quantity
of ripe nectarines.

### raspberry cloud pie
Prepare the basic recipe, replacing the peaches with 3 cups fresh raspberries.
Strain the raspberry mixture through a fine sieve and discard the seeds
before combining the fruit mixture with the gelatin.

### blueberry cloud pie
Prepare the basic recipe, replacing the peaches with 3 cups fresh blueberries.
Strain the blueberry mixture through a fine sieve and discard any solids and
seeds before combining the fruit mixture with the gelatin.

### fresh apricot cloud pie
Prepare the basic recipe, replacing the peaches with an equal quantity
of fresh apricots.

### almond-scented peach cloud pie
Prepare the basic recipe, adding 1/2 teaspoon almond extract along with the
lemon and sugar.

# blueberry-yogurt cream pie

see base recipe page 89

### raspberry-yogurt cream pie
Prepare the basic recipe, replacing the blueberries with 2 cups fresh raspberries.

### strawberry-yogurt cream pie
Prepare the basic recipe, replacing the blueberries with 2 cups hulled
and halved strawberries.

### cherry-yogurt cream pie
Prepare the basic recipe, replacing the blueberries with 2 cups pitted cherries.

### blueberry-yogurt cream pie in gingersnap crust
Prepare the basic recipe, replacing the basic crumb crust with the gingersnap
crumb crust variation (page 22).

variations

# chocolate cream tart

see base recipe page 90

### mocha cream tart
Prepare the basic recipe, adding 2 teaspoons instant coffee powder to the
sugar and cornstarch mixture before adding the milk.

### chocolate cream tart with basic crust
Prepare the basic recipe, replacing the chocolate wafer crumb crust with
a prebaked 1/2 recipe basic crust (page 18).

### chocolate-hazelnut cream tart
Prepare the basic recipe, replacing the melted chocolates with 2/3 cup
chocolate-hazelnut spread. Reduce the sugar to 1/3 cup.

### white chocolate cream tart
Prepare the basic recipe, replacing the melted chocolates with 7 oz. good
quality white chocolate, such as Lindt or Baker's. Reduce the sugar to 1/3 cup.

### chocolate-mint cream tart
Prepare the basic recipe, omitting the vanilla extract and replacing it with
1/2 teaspoon peppermint extract. Garnish with chopped Andes Crème de
Menthe Candies.

variations

# pink grapefruit custard tart

see base recipe page 92

### seville orange custard tart
Prepare the basic recipe, replacing the grapefruit juice with an equal quantity of juice from Seville oranges. Increase the sugar to 1 cup. Serve with sweet orange segments.

### pink rhubarb custard tart
Prepare the basic recipe, replacing the pink grapefruit juice with juice from stewed rhubarb. Prepare stewed rhubarb by cooking 4 cups sliced pink rhubarb with 1 cup sugar over medium heat for 10 minutes, or until the rhubarb softens. Strain the rhubarb through a fine sieve, collecting the juice in a measuring cup. Serve the tart with the reserved stewed rhubarb.

### pink grapefruit custard tart with hazelnut crust
Prepare the basic recipe, replacing the basic sweet crust with the hazelnut sweet crust variation (page 21).

### pink grapefruit custard tart with candied ginger
Prepare the basic recipe, omitting the roasted grapefruit segments and garnishing with 2 tablespoons minced candied ginger.

variations

# lemon mousse pie

see base recipe page 93

### orange mousse pie
Prepare the basic recipe, replacing the lemon juice with fresh orange juice and the zest of 1 lemon with the zest of 1/2 an orange. Reduce the sugar to 1/2 cup, using only 1/4 cup with the orange juice and zest.

### lime mousse pie
Prepare the basic recipe, replacing the lemon juice with lime juice, and the zest of 1 lemon with the zest of 1 lime.

### coffee mousse pie
Prepare the basic recipe, omitting the lemon juice and zest. Dissolve 4 teaspoons instant coffee powder and an additional 1/4 cup sugar in 3 tablespoons boiling water. Proceed with the recipe.

### lemon mousse pie with chocolate wafer crumb crust
Prepare the basic recipe, replacing the basic crumb crust with the chocolate wafer crumb crust (page 22).

### light lemon mousse pie
Prepare the basic recipe, replacing the basic crumb crust with the light crumb crust (page 23). Substitute 1/3 cup light ricotta cheese and 1/3 cup light cream cheese, softened, for the whipping cream. Proceed with recipe.

variations

# banana cream pie

see base recipe page 94

### banana chocolate chip cream pie
Prepare the basic recipe, sprinkling 1/4 cup semisweet chocolate chips over each layer of banana slices.

### banana cream pie with gingersnap crumb crust
Prepare the basic recipe, replacing the basic crumb crust with a prebaked gingersnap crumb crust (page 22).

### banana cream pie with caramel drizzle
Prepare the basic recipe, drizzling 1/4 cup caramel sauce (page 27) in lines across the whipped cream layer.

### banana & strawberry cream pie
Prepare the basic recipe, reducing the amount of banana slices by half and adding 1 cup hulled and halved strawberries. Toss the strawberries with the banana slices in lemon juice.

variations

# maple custard tart

see base recipe page 96

### vanilla–maple custard tart
Prepare the basic recipe, omitting the cinnamon and adding 1 teaspoon vanilla extract to the filling mixture.

### almond–maple custard tart
Prepare the basic recipe, omitting the cinnamon and adding 1 teaspoon almond extract to the filling mixture.

### honey custard tart
Prepare the basic recipe, replacing the maple syrup with an equal quantity of honey.

### banana–maple custard tart
Prepare the basic recipe, arranging a layer of banana slices on the crust before pouring in the filling.

### apple–maple custard tart
Prepare the basic recipe, arranging a layer of apple slices on the crust before pouring in the filling.

variations

# bavarian apple-almond torte

see base recipe page 99

### bavarian pear-almond torte
Prepare the basic recipe, replacing the apple slices in the topping with
an equal quantity of Bosc or Anjou pear slices.

### bavarian apricot-almond torte
Prepare the basic recipe, replacing the apple slices in the topping with
an equal quantity of fresh apricot slices.

### bavarian raspberry-almond torte
Prepare the basic recipe, replacing the apple slices in the topping with
3 cups fresh raspberries. Omit the cinnamon in the topping.

### bavarian apple-walnut torte
Prepare the basic recipe, replacing the sliced almonds with 1/4 cup
chopped walnuts.

### bavarian sour cherry–almond torte
Prepare the basic recipe, replacing the apple slices with 2 cups
pitted sour cherries.

variations

# raspberry chiffon pavlova

see base recipe page 100

### blueberry chiffon pavlova
Prepare the basic recipe, replacing the frozen raspberries with an equal quantity of frozen blueberries. Garnish with fresh blueberries.

### lemon chiffon pavlova
Prepare the basic recipe, replacing the raspberry chiffon with the lemon mousse from Lemon Mousse Pie (page 93). Garnish with strips of lemon zest.

### peach chiffon pavlova
Prepare the basic recipe, replacing the raspberry chiffon with the peach chiffon filling from Peach Cloud Pie (page 87). Garnish with peach slices.

### chocolate chiffon pavlova
Prepare the basic recipe, replacing the raspberry chiffon with the chocolate filling from Chocolate Cream Tart (page 90). Garnish with chocolate shavings.

### strawberry chiffon pavlova
Prepare the basic recipe, replacing the frozen raspberries with an equal quantity of frozen strawberries. Garnish with the strawberry slices.

variations

# butterscotch chiffon pie

see base recipe page 103

### chocolate-butterscotch chiffon pie
Prepare the basic recipe, replacing the 1/2 recipe basic crust with a
prebaked chocolate wafer crumb crust variation (page 22). Garnish
with chocolate shavings.

### butterscotch pie with pecan crunch topping
Prepare the basic recipe. Make pecan crunch topping by toasting 1 cup
chopped pecans in 1 tablespoon unsalted butter with a pinch of salt. Cook
over medium heat for 5 minutes, until the nuts start to turn golden. Cool
completely and sprinkle over the butterscotch filling.

### pumpkin chiffon pie
Prepare the basic recipe, replacing the butterscotch with 1 cup pumpkin pie
filling. Fold in the whipped cream and egg whites into the pumpkin.

### butterscotch chiffon pie with shortbread crumb crust
Prepare the basic recipe, replacing the 1/2 recipe basic crust with the
shortbread crumb crust variation (page 23).

# meringue, frozen & chilled pies

When it is too hot to turn on the oven, try one of these frozen or chilled pies for dessert. With little or no baking involved, they are the perfect choice for a summer day.

# key lime pie

see variations page 132

This Florida pie can be made with other varieties of limes if key limes are not available. Ensure this pie is chilled before serving, as the lime flavor intensifies when it is cold.

1/2 recipe basic crust (page 18)
3 large egg yolks
14-oz. can sweetened condensed milk
zest of 1 key lime
1/2 cup key lime juice (approx. 4 limes)

3 large egg whites
1/2 tsp. vanilla extract
1/4 tsp. cream of tartar
6 tbsp. superfine sugar

Preheat the oven to 425°F (220°C). Roll out the pastry dough and line a 9-in. (23-cm.) pie plate. Crimp the edge decoratively and prick the bottom and sides with a fork. Prebake for 15 minutes. Transfer to a wire rack to cool.

Lower the temperature to 325°F (160°C). Beat the egg yolks, condensed milk, lime zest, and juice until well combined. Pour the lime filling into the crust and bake for 35 minutes, or until the center of the filling is set. Transfer to a wire rack to cool.

Increase the oven temperature to 350°F (175°C). To prepare the meringue, beat the egg whites, vanilla, and cream of tartar using an electric mixer. Beat in the sugar a tablespoon at a time. Continue beating until soft peaks form. Top the pie with the meringue and bake for 12 to 15 minutes, until the peaks of meringue are golden brown. Transfer to a wire rack to cool. Chill in the refrigerator until ready to serve, at least 2 hours. Refrigerate any remaining pie for up to 3 days.

*Serves 6-8*

# retro rum-raisin meringue pie

see variations page 133

This pie evokes that favorite flavor combination of the '70s — rum and raisin.

1/2 recipe basic crust (page 18)
1/3 cup golden raisins
3 tbsp. rum
1 tbsp. granulated sugar
1 tbsp. cornstarch
1/2 tsp. cinnamon
1/2 tsp. nutmeg

1/8 tsp. salt
1 2/3 cups whipping cream
4 large egg yolks, beaten
3 large egg whites
1/4 tsp. cream of tartar
1/2 tsp. vanilla extract
1/3 cup superfine sugar

Preheat the oven to 425°F (220°C). Roll out the pastry dough and line a 9-in. (23-cm.) pie plate. Prick the surface with a fork and prebake for 15 minutes. Transfer to a wire rack to cool. Lower the temperature to 350°F (175°C). Place the raisins in a small bowl with the rum. Stir to coat evenly, set aside for 30 minutes. Combine the granulated sugar, cornstarch, cinnamon, nutmeg, and salt in a double boiler. Over low heat, slowly whisk in 1/3 cup of the cream until smooth. Add the remaining cream. Cook, whisking often, until the mixture thickens. Remove from heat. Slowly whisk in the egg yolks and return to low heat, cooking until the mixture thickens more, but does not boil. Remove from heat. Stir in the rum and raisins. Press parchment paper over the surface to prevent a skin from forming. Cool completely. To make the meringue, beat the egg whites, cream of tartar, and vanilla with an electric mixer on high. When it becomes foamy, begin adding the superfine sugar, 1 tablespoon at a time. Continue beating until stiff peaks form. Pour the rum and raisin mixture into the crust. Top with the meringue and bake for 12 to 15 minutes, until the meringue peaks turn golden brown. Transfer to a wire rack to cool. Serve warm or cold. Refrigerate any remaining pie for up to 3 days.

*Serves 6–8*

# mud pie

see variations page 134

This pie is named after the muddy waters of the Mississippi River.

1 recipe chocolate wafer crumb crust variation
  (page 22)
2 cups chocolate ice cream,
  slightly softened

1 1/2 cups hot fudge sauce, store-bought
  or homemade (page 26)
1/4 cup chopped almonds, lightly toasted

Preheat the oven to 350°F (175°C). Press the chocolate wafer crumb crust into a 9-in. (23-cm.) pie plate. Bake for 15 minutes. Transfer to a wire rack and cool completely.

Spoon the softened ice cream over the piecrust and smooth the top.

Spread the hot fudge sauce over the ice cream layer and garnish with toasted almonds. Cover loosely with plastic wrap, using toothpicks to prevent the plastic from sticking to the sauce. Freeze for 4 hours or until firm.

Remove from the freezer 15 minutes prior to serving, to allow the pie to soften.

Freeze any remaining pie.

*Serves 6–8*

# rhubarb meringue pie

see variations page 135

A mouthwatering way to celebrate the arrival of spring.

1/2 recipe basic crust (page 18)
2 large eggs
1 cup granulated sugar
1/3 cup all-purpose flour
4 cups rhubarb, cut into 1/2-in.
   (1.5-cm.) pieces

2 tbsp. unsalted butter, for dotting
3 large egg whites
1/2 tsp. vanilla extract
1/4 tsp. cream of tartar
6 tbsp. superfine sugar

Preheat the oven to 425°F (220°C). Roll out the pastry dough and line a 9-in. (23-cm.) pie plate. Prick the surface with a fork and prebake for 15 minutes. Cool on a wire rack.

Lower the temperature to 375°F (190°C). Using an electric mixer, beat the eggs and granulated sugar until the mixture thickens. Add the flour and rhubarb and stir to combine. Pour into the cooled piecrust and dot with butter. Bake for 40 minutes, or until the filling is bubbling and the rhubarb is tender. Transfer to a wire rack to cool.

To prepare the meringue, beat the egg whites, vanilla, and cream of tartar until foamy using an electric mixer. Add the superfine sugar a tablespoon at a time, while beating constantly until soft peaks form. Top the pie with the meringue and bake for 12 to 15 minutes, until the meringue peaks are golden brown. Transfer to a wire rack to cool.

*Serves 6–8*

# chocolate strata pie

see variations page 136

This decadent pie is named for its four delectable layers of chocolate.

1 recipe chocolate wafer crumb crust (page 22)
3 1/2 cups whipping cream
4 oz. unsweetened chocolate, finely chopped
1 cup semisweet chocolate chips
1/2 tsp. vanilla extract

pinch of salt
3 large egg whites
1/4 tsp. cream of tartar
1/3 cup superfine sugar
2 tsp. unsweetened, Dutch-process cocoa

Preheat the oven to 350°F (175°C). Press the crust into a 9-in. (23-cm.) pie plate. Bake for 15 minutes. Transfer to a wire rack to cool. In a saucepan bring 1/2 cup of the cream to a boil. To make the ganache, place the unsweetened chocolate in a bowl and pour the hot cream over it – stir until it has melted and the ganache is smooth. Cool for 30 minutes. Spread over the crust and chill for 2 hours. Bring 1 cup cream to a boil in a heavy saucepan. Place the chocolate chips in a bowl and pour the hot cream over them, stirring until they have melted. Stir in the vanilla and salt. Cool completely.

Using an electric mixer beat the last 2 cups of cream until stiff. Gently fold into the cooled, melted chocolate mixture until well combined. Pour this chocolate mousse over the ganache and chill for 2 hours. Beat the egg whites and cream of tartar. When the egg whites foam, begin adding the sugar a tablespoon at a time. Continue beating until stiff peaks form. Spoon the meringue over the chocolate mousse, using the back of a spoon to form peaks. Use a chef's blowtorch to lightly brown the meringue. Dust the meringue with cocoa powder.

*Serves 6–8*

# banana & strawberry split pie ✐

see variations page 137

This easy-to-assemble dessert takes all the ingredients from the classic sundae and turns it into a kid-friendly summer pie.

1 recipe basic crumb crust (page 22)
1 1/2 cups hot fudge sauce, store-bought or
   homemade (page 26)
2 large bananas, sliced
2 cups vanilla ice cream, slightly softened

1 cup whipping cream
2 tbsp. confectioners' sugar
2 cups strawberries, sliced
1 banana and a handful of strawberries,
   sliced, to decorate

Preheat the oven to 350°F (175°C). Press the crumb crust into a 9-in. (23-cm.) pie plate. Bake for 15 minutes. Transfer to a wire rack and cool completely.

Pour 1 cup of the hot fudge sauce over the cooled piecrust. Arrange the sliced bananas on top. Spoon the softened ice cream over the bananas and smooth the top. Cover the pie with plastic wrap and freeze for 3 hours.

Using an electric mixer, beat the cream and confectioners' sugar until stiff peaks form. Arrange the sliced strawberries over the ice cream filling and spoon the whipped cream on top.

Scatter the banana and strawberry slices on top to decorate. Warm the remaining 1/2 cup hot fudge sauce in a small saucepan over low heat and drizzle over the whipped cream and fruit. Freeze any remaining pie for up to 3 days.

*Serves 6–8*

# chocolate silk pie

see variations page 138

A chocolate pie that is as smooth as silk — how can you go wrong?

1/2 recipe basic crust (page 18)
4 oz. unsweetened baking chocolate
1/4 cup unsalted butter
1 cup granulated sugar
3 tbsp. cornstarch

3 large eggs
1 1/2 tsp. vanilla extract
2 cups whipping cream
1 tbsp. confectioners' sugar
1 oz. semisweet chocolate, melted

Preheat the oven to 425°F (220°C). Roll out the pastry dough and line a 9-in. (23-cm.) pie plate. Prick the surface with a fork and prebake for 20 minutes or until the crust is golden. Transfer to a wire rack to cool.

Melt the chocolate and butter in a double boiler. Remove from heat. Combine the sugar and cornstarch, add to the chocolate mixture, and stir until smooth. Using an electric mixer, beat the eggs on medium until they become light yellow and thick. Stir the eggs into the chocolate mixture and return to medium heat. Cook for 5 minutes, stirring constantly, until the mixture thickens and becomes glossy. Whisk in the vanilla. Remove from heat and cool completely. Using an electric mixer, beat 1 cup of the cream until stiff. Incorporate the chocolate mixture into the whipped cream, folding gently. Spread the filling evenly over the baked crust. Cover with plastic wrap and chill for 4 hours. Use an electric mixer to beat the remaining 1 cup cream and the confectioners' sugar until stiff. Top the filling with the whipped cream. To garnish, drizzle melted chocolate in lines over the cream. Refrigerate any remaining pie for up to 3 days.

*Serves 6–8*

# strawberry daiquiri pie

see variations page 139

Summer dessert meets cocktail hour!

1 recipe basic crumb crust (page 22)
3 cups strawberries, hulled and halved
1 tbsp. lime zest
1/4 cup fresh lime juice
14-oz. can sweetened condensed milk

3 tbsp. rum
2 tbsp. Cointreau (optional)
1 1/2 cups whipping cream
sliced strawberries, for garnish

Preheat the oven to 350°F (175°C). Press the crumb crust into a 9-in. (23-cm.) pie plate. Bake for 15 minutes. Transfer to a wire rack to cool.

To make the filling, use a blender or food processor to purée the strawberries, lime zest and juice, condensed milk, rum, and Cointreau (if using) until smooth. Using an electric mixer, beat the cream on high until stiff peaks form.

Transfer the strawberry mixture to a large bowl and gently fold in the whipped cream, 1/2 cup at a time, until well combined. Pour the filling into the crust, smoothing the top. Cover the pie with plastic wrap and freeze for 3 hours.

Let the pie sit at room temperature for 30 minutes before serving, to soften. Garnish the pie with sliced strawberries. Freeze any remaining pie for up to 1 week.

*Serves 6–8*

# cranberry-orange smoothie pie

see variations page 140

This frozen pie is a wonderful way to get your daily dose of vitamin C!

1 recipe basic crumb crust (page 22)
1 envelope unflavored gelatin
1/3 cup cranberry juice

3 cups fresh orange segments
2 cups plain yogurt
fresh mint leaves, for garnish

Preheat the oven to 350°F (175°C). Press the crumb crust into a 9-in. (23-cm.) pie plate and bake for 15 minutes. Transfer to a wire rack to cool.

To make the filling, sprinkle the gelatin over the cranberry juice in a small saucepan. Set aside for 5 minutes. Cook the gelatin and juice over medium heat for 3 to 4 minutes, whisking constantly, until the gelatin has dissolved and the mixture begins to thicken. Remove from heat and cool completely.

Using a blender or food processor, blend the gelatin mixture, oranges, and yogurt until smooth. Pour the filling into the cooled piecrust. Cover the pie with plastic wrap and freeze for 4 hours, or until set. Garnish with fresh mint leaves.

Freeze any remaining pie for up to 1 week.

*Serves 6–8*

# grasshopper pie

see variations page 141

The flavors of mint and chocolate blend spectacularly in this spiked chilled pie.

1 recipe chocolate wafer crumb crust variation
    (page 22)
1 1/2 tsp. unflavored gelatin
1 1/3 cups whipping cream
1/4 cup superfine sugar
3 tbsp. crème de menthe

1/4 cup white crème de cacao
4 large egg yolks
Rough chopped Andes Crème de Menthe
    Candies, or shavings from other mint-
    chocolate candy bar

Preheat the oven to 350°F (175°C). Press the crust into a 9-in. (23-cm.) pie plate and bake for 15 minutes. Transfer to a wire rack to cool. Sprinkle the gelatin over 1/3 cup of the cream in a large saucepan and set aside for a few minutes while you fill a large bowl with ice and cold water.

Using a whisk, combine the sugar, crème de menthe, crème de cacao, and egg yolks in the saucepan with the gelatin and cook over medium-low heat for 3 to 4 minutes, stirring continuously until the gelatin has dissolved. Pour the gelatin mixture into a metal bowl and set the bowl in the ice bath. Chill, stirring occasionally, for 10 to 15 minutes, until the mixture begins to thicken, leaving a mound when dropped from a spoon. Using an electric mixer, beat the remaining 1 cup cream until stiff peaks form. Gently fold the cream into the gelatin mixture, 1/3 cup at a time, until well combined. Pour the filling into the cooled crust and refrigerate for 3 hours, or until the filling has set. Garnish with the chopped or shaved candy bar. Refrigerate any remaining pie for up to 3 days.

*Serves 6–8*

variations

# key lime pie

see base recipe page 115

### key lime pie with whipped cream topping
Prepare the basic recipe, omitting the meringue topping and replacing with basic whipped cream (page 25). Chill for 2 hours.

### key lime pie in crumb crust
Prepare the basic recipe, replacing the basic crust with a prebaked basic crumb crust (page 22).

### key lime tart with chocolate crust
Prepare the basic recipe, replacing the basic crust with a prebaked chocolate sweet crust variation (page 21). Garnish with unsweetened chocolate shavings.

### light key lime raspberry pie
Prepare the basic recipe, replacing the basic crust with a prebaked light crumb crust (page 23). Substitute lowfat sweetened condensed milk in the filling. Omit the meringue topping and garnish with fresh raspberries.

### key lime pie with kiwi coulis
Prepare the basic recipe. Garnish with kiwi slices and serve with a drizzle of kiwi coulis (page 27).

variations

# retro rum-raisin meringue pie

see base recipe page 117

**brandy-raisin meringue pie**
Prepare the basic recipe, replacing the rum with 3 tablespoons brandy.

**rum-cranberry meringue pie**
Prepare the basic recipe, replacing the golden raisins with an equal quantity
of dried cranberries.

**rum-apricot meringue pie**
Prepare the basic recipe, replacing the golden raisins with an equal quantity
of chopped dried apricots.

**rum-raisin cardamom meringue pie**
Prepare the basic recipe, adding 1/2 teaspoon cardamom with the cinnamon
and nutmeg.

variations

# mud pie

see base recipe page 118

### mocha mud pie
Prepare the basic recipe, replacing the chocolate ice cream with 2 cups coffee ice cream.

### heavenly mud pie
Prepare the basic recipe, replacing the chocolate ice cream with 2 cups heavenly hash ice cream.

### mud pie with whipped cream topping
Prepare the basic recipe, topping the hot fudge sauce with basic whipped cream (page 25). Garnish with toasted almonds.

### mud pie with pecan crunch topping
Prepare the basic recipe. Omit the toasted almonds. Make the pecan crunch topping by toasting 1 cup chopped pecans in 1 tablespoon unsalted butter with a pinch of salt. Cook over medium heat for 5 minutes, until the nuts start to turn golden. Cool completely and sprinkle over the hot fudge sauce.

### vanilla ice cream pie
Prepare the basic recipe, replacing the chocolate ice cream with an equal quantity of vanilla ice cream.

variations

# rhubarb meringue pie

see base recipe page 119

### rhubarb-orange meringue pie
Prepare the basic recipe, adding the zest and juice of 1 large orange to the filling with the rhubarb.

### rhubarb-ginger meringue pie
Prepare the basic recipe, adding 1/4 cup candied ginger to the filling with the rhubarb.

### rhubarb-strawberry meringue pie
Prepare the basic recipe, reducing the amount of rhubarb to 3 cups, and adding 1 cup hulled and halved strawberries to the filling with the rhubarb.

### rhubarb meringue pie with citrus crust
Prepare the basic recipe, replacing the 1/2 recipe basic crust with 1/2 recipe citrus crust variation (page 19).

variations

# chocolate strata pie

see base recipe page 120

### black forest strata pie
Prepare the basic recipe, adding 2 teaspoons Kirsch to the unsweetened chocolate ganache mixture. Fold 1 cup drained, pitted sour cherries into the chocolate mousse mixture.

### chocolate raspberry strata pie
Prepare the basic recipe, adding 2 teaspoons raspberry liqueur (such as Chambord) to the unsweetened chocolate ganache. Arrange a layer of 1 cup fresh raspberries over the ganache and proceed with the recipe.

### chocolate strata tart
Prepare the basic recipe, replacing the chocolate wafer crumb crust with a prebaked chocolate sweet crust variation (page 21) in an 11-in. (28-cm.) fluted tart pan.

### chocolate strata pie with cocoa-dusted whipped cream topping
Prepare the basic recipe, replacing the meringue topping with basic whipped cream (page 25). Dust with cocoa.

variations

# banana & strawberry split pie

see base recipe page 123

### banana & strawberry split pie with pineapple
Prepare the basic recipe, adding 1 cup drained, crushed pineapple over the ice cream topping.

### banana & strawberry split pie with chocolate wafer crumb crust
Prepare the basic recipe, replacing the basic crumb crust with the chocolate wafer crumb crust variation (page 22).

### banana & strawberry split pie with pecan crunch topping
Prepare the basic recipe. Make the pecan crunch topping by toasting 1 cup chopped pecans in 1 tablespoon unsalted butter with a pinch of salt. Cook over medium heat for 5 minutes, until the nuts start to turn golden. Cool completely and sprinkle over the whipped cream topping.

### banana & strawberry split pie with butterscotch sauce
Prepare the basic recipe, replacing the hot fudge sauce with 1 1/2 cups butterscotch sauce (page 27).

### banana & strawberry split pie with cherries on top
Prepare the basic recipe, arranging 1/2 cup maraschino cherries over the whipped cream topping.

variations

# chocolate silk pie

see base recipe page 124

### mocha silk pie
Prepare the basic recipe, adding 2 teaspoons instant coffee granules to the melted chocolate mixture.

### chocolate silk pie in chocolate wafer crumb crust
Prepare the basic recipe, replacing the 1/2 recipe basic crust with a prebaked chocolate wafer crumb crust (page 22).

### white chocolate silk pie
Prepare the basic recipe, replacing the unsweetened chocolate with 4 oz. white bakers' chocolate. Reduce the sugar to 1/4 cup.

### butterscotch silk pie
Prepare the basic recipe, replacing the unsweetened chocolate with 1 cup butterscotch chips. Reduce the sugar to 1/4 cup.

variations

# strawberry daiquiri pie

see base recipe page 127

### strawberry margarita pie
Prepare the basic recipe, replacing the Cointreau with an equal quantity
of tequila.

### strawberry daiquiri pie with whipped cream topping
Prepare the basic recipe, covering the filling with basic whipped cream
topping (page 25). Garnish with strawberries.

### raspberry daiquiri pie
Prepare the basic recipe, replacing the strawberries with 2 cups raspberries.

### peach daiquiri pie
Prepare the basic recipe, replacing the strawberries with 3 cups
sliced peaches.

variations

# cranberry-orange smoothie pie

see base recipe page 128

### strawberry-orange smoothie pie
Prepare the basic recipe, replacing the cranberry juice with 1/3 cup orange juice. Replace the orange segments with 3 cups hulled and halved fresh strawberries.

### peach-raspberry smoothie pie
Prepare the basic recipe, replacing the cranberry juice with peach nectar. Replace the orange segments with 3 cups fresh raspberries.

### cranberry-orange smoothie pie in shortbread crumb crust
Prepare the basic recipe, replacing the basic crumb crust with the shortbread crumb crust variation (page 23).

### light cranberry-orange smoothie pie
Prepare the basic recipe, replacing the basic crumb crust with the light crumb crust variation (page 23). Use reduced-calorie cranberry juice and low-fat yogurt.

variations

# grasshopper pie

see base recipe page 131

### grasshopper tart in confectioners' sugar sweet crust
Prepare the basic recipe, replacing the chocolate wafer crumb crust
with a fully baked confectioners' sugar sweet crust variation in a 10-in.
(25-cm.) fluted tart pan.

### grasshopper pie with mint whipped cream topping
Prepare the basic recipe. Whisk 1 tablespoon crème de menthe into 1 cup
whipped cream and spoon decoratively over the pie. Garnish with fresh
mint leaves.

### irish cream pie
Prepare the basic recipe, omitting the crème de menthe and crème de cacao.
Add 1/3 cup Bailey's Irish Cream liqueur with the sugar and egg yolks.

# savory pies
# & tarts

Savory pies and tarts can range from

pure comfort food to elegant fare for

a luncheon or dinner party.

# summer vegetable tart

see variations page 160

Made with fresh, vine-ripened tomatoes, zucchini, and fragrant pesto, this tart
has all of summer's signature flavors.

1/2 recipe basic crust (page 18)
2 1/2 lb. cherry tomatoes, still on the vine
1 tbsp. balsamic vinegar
1 egg, lightly beaten
1 medium red onion, sliced
1 tbsp. olive oil

2 garlic cloves, minced
1 small zucchini, sliced
3 tbsp. pesto
2 cups baby bocconcini, sliced
fresh basil leaves
freshly ground black pepper

Preheat the oven to 400°F (200°C). Remove the cherry tomatoes from the vine and place in
a roasting pan. Drizzle balsamic vinegar over the tomatoes and roast for 45 minutes, or until
the tomatoes are soft and lightly charred. Transfer to a wire rack to cool. Roll out the pastry
and line an 11-in. (28-cm.) tart pan. Prick the surface with a fork and chill for 10 minutes
in the freezer. Bake blind for 20 minutes. Remove and brush the tart base with the egg.
Return to the oven for 10 minutes. Transfer to wire rack to cool. Lower the temperature to
350°F (175°C). In a skillet, fry the onion in olive oil for 10 minutes, until it becomes soft. Add
the garlic and zucchini and fry for 3 to 5 minutes longer, until the zucchini is crisp-tender.
Remove from heat. To assemble the tart, spread the onion and zucchini mixture over the
base of the tart. Layer the roasted tomatoes on top. Drizzle the pesto over the tomatoes.
Arrange the bocconcini slices over the pesto. Bake for 25 minutes, or until the bocconcini
have melted and turned golden brown. Transfer to a wire rack to cool for 10 minutes. Serve
warm. Garnish with basil leaves and black pepper.

*Serves 4–6*

# chicken pot pie

see variations page 161

The perfect way to use up leftover roast chicken, this pot pie is pure comfort food.

| | |
|---|---|
| 1/2 recipe basic crust (page 18) | 2 tbsp. all-purpose flour |
| 1 large potato, peeled and cut into small cubes | 2 1/4 cups whole milk |
| 2 carrots, peeled and cut into small chunks | 1/2 cup frozen peas |
| 2 tbsp. salted butter | 2 cups cooked chicken |
| 1 chicken stock cube | freshly ground black pepper, to taste |

Preheat the oven to 375°F (190°C). Place the potato and carrots in a saucepan filled with water. Bring to a boil and cook the vegetables for 5 to 10 minutes, until tender but not soft. Remove from heat, drain, and set aside. In a medium saucepan, melt the butter with the chicken stock cube. Use a wooden spoon to break up the cube. When the butter has melted and the mixture is smooth, add the flour, stirring to form a smooth paste. Cook over low heat for a minute. Remove from the heat and add the milk, stirring constantly. When the mixture is smooth, cook over medium-low heat for 10 minutes, until the sauce thickens. Remove from the heat. Stir in the cooked vegetables, frozen peas, and chicken, and season with pepper. Butter a 9-in. (23-cm.) pie plate and pour in the chicken mixture.

Roll out the pastry dough into a 10-in. (25-cm.) round. Moisten the edge of the pie plate with milk or water. Place the crust over the chicken mixture, pressing the edge down on the pie plate to seal, crimp decoratively, and make 4 to 6 slits in the crust. Bake for 30 minutes or until the filling is hot and the crust is golden brown. Refrigerate any remaining pie for up to 3 days.

*Serves 4–6*

# shepherd's pie

see variations page 162

This hearty pie is topped with mashed potatoes, so there is no pastry involved!

| | |
|---|---|
| 2 lb. ground lamb, browned and drained | 4–5 large russet potatoes |
| 1/2 tsp. dried rosemary, crushed | 6 tbsp. salted butter |
| freshly ground black pepper | 1/2 cup whole milk |
| 1 cup canned or frozen corn | 1/4 tsp. salt |
| | 1 tbsp. chopped fresh flat-leaf parsley |

Preheat the oven to 375°F (190°C). Spread the cooked lamb over the bottom of a buttered, large rectangular baking dish (13 x 9 x 2 in./33 x 22 x 6 cm.). Sprinkle the crushed rosemary and ground pepper over the lamb, and spread the corn over the top.

To make the mashed potatoes, peel and halve the potatoes. Place in a large saucepan and cover with water. Bring to a boil, and cook for 20 minutes, or until the potatoes begin to fall apart when pricked with a fork. Drain the potatoes and mash for a few seconds. Add the butter, milk, salt, and pepper and beat until the potatoes are light and creamy.

Spread the potatoes over the filling. Bake the pie for 20 minutes, or until the potatoes are lightly browned. Garnish with chopped parsley. Refrigerate any remaining pie, covered, for up to 3 days.

*Serves 4–6*

# apple custard tart with camembert & tarragon

see variations page 163

This elegant tart plays on the contrast between the tangy apples and smooth Camembert-flavored custard with impressive results.

1/2 recipe basic crust (page 18)
1 large egg, lightly beaten
3/4 cup (6 oz.) roughly chopped Camembert
   cheese, room temperature
1 large egg
2 large egg yolks

1 cup half-and-half
2 tbsp. chopped fresh tarragon
salt and freshly ground black pepper, to taste
2 tart apples, such as Granny Smith, peeled,
   cored, and sliced thickly

Preheat the oven to 400°F (200°C). Roll out the pastry dough and transfer to a 10-in. (25-cm.) tart pan. Bake blind for 15 minutes. Remove from the oven, prick the surface with a fork, and brush with egg. Bake for 10 minutes longer. Transfer to a wire rack to cool. Place the chopped Camembert in a large bowl. Using an electric mixer, beat until only a few lumps remain. Add the egg and egg yolks, and beat until well combined. Add 1/4 cup of the half-and-half and beat until smooth. Add the remaining half-and-half and beat. Add the tarragon, salt, and pepper and stir until well combined. Arrange the apple slices on the base of the cooled tart shell. Pour the custard over the apples and bake for 35 minutes, or until the custard is set. Transfer to a wire rack to cool for 15 minutes. Serve warm.

Refrigerate any remaining tart for up to 3 days.

*Serves 4-6*

# beef pot pie

see variations page 164

The perfect supper for a cold winter evening.

3/4 recipe basic pie crust (see page 18)
2 1/4 lb. beef, blade, or chuck steak, cut into
    1-in. (3-cm.) pieces
1/4 cup all-purpose flour, for coating beef
2 tbsp. vegetable oil
1 small yellow onion, chopped
2 garlic cloves, minced
1 1/2 tbsp. olive oil

1 celery stalk, diced
2 carrots, peeled and chopped
1 bay leaf
3 tbsp. dry mustard
3 cups beef stock
salt and freshly ground black pepper, to taste
2 tbsp. all-purpose flour
1/2 cup cold water

Preheat the oven to 375°F (190°C). Coat the beef with a light layer of flour. Pour
1 1/2 tablespoons of the vegetable oil into a medium Dutch oven. When the oil is hot,
brown the beef in batches, adding more oil as needed. When all the beef is browned, drain
and set aside. In the Dutch oven, fry the onion and garlic in the olive oil for 2 to 3 minutes,
until the onion begins to soften. Add the celery and carrots and cook for 3 minutes more.
Return the beef to the Dutch oven with the bay leaf, mustard, stock, and salt and pepper.
Bring to a boil, reduce the heat, and simmer, covered, for 30 minutes. Remove the lid and
simmer for 30 minutes more, until the beef is tender. Whisk the flour into 1/2 cup cold
water. When the mixture is smooth, combine with the beef. Cook for 3 to 5 minutes, until
the sauce thickens. Remove from the heat. Roll out the pastry dough to fit the surface of
the Dutch oven. Cover the beef mixture with the crust, pushing the excess down the sides
to seal. Make 4 to 6 slits in the top. Bake uncovered for 25 minutes, or until the filling is hot
and the crust is golden brown.

*Serves 4–6*

# quiche lorraine

see variations page 165

Served with a mixed salad and vinaigrette, this makes a sumptuous lunch or light supper.

1/2 recipe basic crust (page 18)
8 slices bacon
4 large eggs, lightly beaten
1 1/4 cups whipping cream

1/4 tsp. salt
freshly ground black pepper to taste
pinch of nutmeg

Preheat the oven to 425°F (220°C). Roll out the pastry dough and transfer to a 9-in. (23-cm.) pie plate. Prick the surface with a fork and bake for 15 minutes. Transfer to a wire rack to cool. Lower the temperature to 400°F (200°C). Fry the bacon slices in a skillet over medium-high heat until the bacon is beginning to crisp. Remove from the heat and drain on paper towels.

In a large bowl, whisk the eggs with the cream, salt, pepper, and nutmeg until well combined. Chop the bacon and sprinkle over the bottom of the cooled piecrust. Pour the egg and cream mixture over the bacon. Bake for 30 minutes.

Serve hot, warm, or cold. Refrigerate any remaining quiche for up to 3 days.

*Serves 4–6*

# mixed mushroom tart with gruyère & pine nuts

see variations page 166

Served with a fresh green salad, this tart makes a lovely lunch or light supper.

1/2 recipe basic crust (page 18)
1 large egg, lightly beaten
1 head of garlic, unpeeled
1/2 cup ricotta cheese
1/4 cup crème fraiche or sour cream
salt and freshly ground black pepper, to taste

2 tbsp. salted butter
1 tbsp. olive oil
1 1/2 lb. mixed mushrooms, such as oyster, chanterelle, shiitake, and portobello
1/2 cup (4 oz.) grated Gruyère
1/4 cup pine nuts

Preheat the oven to 400°F (200°C). Roll out the pastry dough and transfer to a 9-in. (23-cm.) tart pan. Bake blind for 15 minutes. Remove from the oven, prick the surface with a fork, and brush the surface with lightly beaten egg. Then bake for 10 minutes more. Transfer to a wire rack to cool. Boil a garlic head in a saucepan filled with water for 15 minutes, then drain. When cool enough to handle, pop the garlic cloves out of their skins and mash in a bowl with the ricotta and crème fraiche until smooth. Season with salt and pepper. Heat the butter and olive oil in a skillet and sauté the mushrooms for 10 to 15 minutes, until they are tender and any liquid has evaporated. Season with salt and pepper. To assemble, spread the ricotta and garlic mixture over the base of the cooled tart shell. Layer half of the mushroom mixture, then half of the grated Gruyère. Repeat the mushroom and Gruyère layers and sprinkle the pine nuts over the cheese. Bake for 25 minutes, or until the filling is hot and the pine nuts are golden brown. Refrigerate any remaining pie for up to 3 days.

*Serves 4–6*

# skillet fettuccini pie

see variations page 167

This unusual pie is just right for a casual weeknight supper. It is quick, easy, and delicious — simply serve wedges straight from the skillet.

| | |
|---|---|
| 1 tbsp. olive oil | pinch of cayenne |
| 1 medium onion, sliced | 2 cups canned or frozen corn |
| 2 garlic cloves, minced | salt and freshly ground black pepper |
| 1 medium red bell pepper, chopped | 1/2 lb. uncooked dried fettuccini |
| 4 cups canned, crushed tomatoes | 2/3 cup grated mozzarella |
| 2 tsp. ground cumin | 1/2 cup fresh cilantro, chopped |

Fill a large saucepan with water and bring to a boil. Heat the olive oil in a 10-in. (25-cm.) nonstick skillet. When the oil is hot, add the onion, garlic, and red pepper. Sauté for 10 minutes, until the onion is soft and brown. Add the tomatoes, cumin, cayenne, and corn, and simmer for 5 minutes. Add salt and pepper to taste.

Place the fettuccini in the boiling water and cook for 9 minutes. Drain the pasta and add to the skillet. Taking care to blend the pasta and sauce thoroughly, cook for 10 minutes, until the tomato sauce thickens and coats the pasta evenly. Remove from heat and arrange the grated mozzarella over the pasta. Cover the skillet for several minutes to allow the cheese to melt. Garnish with chopped cilantro.

**QUICK & EASY SHORTCUT:** Fastest Skillet Fettuccini Pie variation page 167.

*Serves 4–6*

# curried garbanzo & currant phyllo pie

see variations page 168

This Middle Eastern–inspired pie is wonderful served with chutney and a mixed salad.

2 tbsp. olive oil
1 small onion, chopped
1/2 tsp. ground cumin
1/2 tsp. turmeric
1 tsp. ground coriander
1/2 cup basmati rice

1 1/4 cups vegetable stock
1/2 cup dried currants or raisins
19-oz. can garbanzo beans, drained
1/2 cup unsalted butter, melted
10 sheets phyllo dough, thawed if frozen

Preheat the oven to 400°F (200°C). To make the filling, heat the olive oil in a large, heavy-based saucepan. Add the onion, reduce the heat, and fry for 5 minutes, until soft. Add the spices and stir to combine. Add the rice and stir to coat evenly with oil. Add the vegetable stock, 1/4 cup at a time, allowing the rice to absorb the liquid. Then add the currants. When the rice is cooked and the currants are plump, remove from the heat. Stir in the garbanzo beans and adjust the seasoning as necessary. Brush a 9-in. (23-cm.) pie plate with melted butter. Layer 6 sheets of phyllo in the pie plate, brushing each one with melted butter, leaving the corners hanging over the edges. Spoon the filling into the pie plate. Fold the overhanging phyllo on top so the filling is completely covered. Brush the remaining 4 sheets of phyllo with butter and place over the top of the pie. Carefully lift the edges of the pie from the plate to fold the corners under. Bake for 25 minutes, until the filling is hot and the pastry is golden. Refrigerate any remaining pie for up to 3 days.

*Serves 4–6*

# carrot & mint custard tart

see variations page 169

Serve this luscious savory tart as a vegetarian appetizer or as an accompaniment to roasted dishes. Try to use organic carrots, as they are more flavorful.

1/2 recipe basic crust (page 18)
1 large egg, lightly beaten
1 tbsp. salted butter
1 tbsp. olive oil
1 large yellow onion, finely chopped
1 garlic clove, minced
1 1/2 lb. organic carrots, chopped
2 tbsp. fresh lemon juice

1 tsp. dried mint
1 tsp. granulated sugar
1/2 tsp. salt
freshly ground black pepper
1/2 cup whipping cream
1 large egg
1 large egg yolk
fresh mint leaves

Preheat the oven to 400°F (200°C). Roll out the pastry dough and line a 9-in. (23-cm.) tart pan. Prick the surface with a fork and chill for 10 minutes in the freezer. Bake blind for 20 minutes. Remove from the oven and brush the base of the tart with lightly beaten egg. Return to the oven for 10 minutes. Transfer to a wire rack to cool. Heat the butter and olive oil in a heavy-bottomed saucepan. When the oil is hot, add the onion and garlic and sauté for 10 minutes over low heat. Steam the carrots for 10 to 15 minutes, until soft. Add the carrots to the onions. Stir in the lemon juice, mint, sugar, and salt and pepper. Cook over low heat for 2 minutes. Remove from the heat. Add 1/4 cup of the cream to the carrot mixture. Using a handheld blender, carefully purée the carrot mixture until smooth. Set aside. Whisk the egg and egg yolk together with the remaining 1/4 cup cream. Combine with the carrot purée. Spoon the filling into the crust and bake for 25 minutes, or until the filling is set. Garnish with fresh mint leaves and serve warm.

*Serves 4–6*

variations

# summer vegetable tart

see base recipe page 143

### summer vegetable tart with chèvre
Prepare the basic recipe, replacing the baby bocconcini with 2 cups sliced soft goat cheese.

### summer vegetable tart with black olives
Prepare the basic recipe, layering 12 pitted black olives (kalamata) over the bocconcini.

### summer vegetable tart with asparagus
Prepare the basic recipe, replacing the zucchini slices with 1/2 lb. asparagus, cut into 2-in. (5-cm.) lengths.

### winter vegetable tart with feta
Prepare the basic recipe, replacing the tomatoes with 2 1/2 lb. roasted butternut squash. Replace the zucchini with 1 large red bell pepper, chopped. Place the roasted squash flesh in a medium bowl and stir in 1 large egg and 1/2 cup buttermilk. Combine the squash mixture with the onion and pepper. Spread the mixture over the base of the tart and spread 1 cup crumbled feta cheese over the filling. Bake for 25 minutes. Garnish with freshly ground black pepper and chopped fresh parsley.

variations

# chicken pot pie

see base recipe page 145

### turkey pot pie
Prepare the basic recipe, replacing the cooked chicken with cooked turkey.

### salmon pot pie
Prepare the basic recipe, replacing the chicken stock cube with a fish or
vegetable stock cube. Replace the chicken with 2 cups cooked, flaked salmon.

### easy chicken pot pie
Prepare the basic recipe, replacing the homemade stock sauce with a 10-oz.
can condensed cream of chicken soup. Whisk in 1 cup whole milk. Remove
from heat; stir in the chicken and 2 cups frozen vegetable mix. Top with
1 sheet rolled out store-bought puff pastry. Make 4 to 6 slits in the top and
bake for 30 minutes, until the filling is hot and the pastry is golden brown.

### chicken & bacon pot pie
Prepare the basic recipe, adding 6 slices bacon, fried and crumbled, to the
filling with the chicken. Add 1 teaspoon dried oregano leaves to the filling.

### chicken & leek pot pie
Prepare the basic recipe, adding 3 medium leeks, white and pale green
parts sliced, to the potatoes and carrots once the water has boiled. Add
1 tablespoon chopped fresh thyme to the filling.

variations

# shepherd's pie

see base recipe page 146

### cottage pie
Prepare the basic recipe, replacing the ground lamb with 2 lb. ground beef, browned and drained.

### shepherd's pie with green peas
Prepare the basic recipe, replacing the corn with 1 cup fresh or frozen peas.

### vegetarian shepherd's pie
Prepare the basic recipe, replacing the ground lamb with 4 cups prepared textured vegetable protein (TVP).

### shepherd's pie with ricotta topping
Prepare the basic recipe, omitting the mashed potato. Combine 2 cups fresh ricotta cheese, 2 large eggs, 1/2 teaspoon dried oregano, and 1/3 cup grated mozzarella cheese in a bowl. Spread over the filling and bake for 20 minutes.

### shepherd's pie with parsnip and potato topping
Prepare the basic recipe, using only 2 large potatoes. Chop 4 large parsnips, removing the tough center. Boil the potatoes and parsnips for 20 minutes and proceed with the recipe.

# apple custard tart with camembert & tarragon

see base recipe page 148

### apple custard tart with chèvre
Prepare the basic recipe, replacing the Camembert with an equal quantity of soft goat cheese. Replace the tart apples with sweet ones.

### asparagus custard tart with camembert & tarragon
Prepare the basic recipe, replacing the apples with 1/2 lb. blanched asparagus. To blanch the asparagus, place the spears, with the tough ends removed, in boiling water for 1 to 2 minutes, until the green color intensifies and the asparagus is crisp-tender.

### apple custard tart with brie & tarragon
Prepare the basic recipe, replacing the Camembert with Brie.

### apple custard tart with camembert & thyme
Prepare the basic recipe, replacing the tarragon with 2 teaspoons chopped fresh thyme.

### apple custard tart with cheddar & tarragon
Prepare the basic recipe, replacing the Camembert with an equal quantity of coarsely grated aged cheddar.

variations

# beef pot pie

see base recipe page 149

### beef & potato pot pie
Prepare the basic recipe, adding 1 large potato, cubed, to the beef mixture when you uncover the Dutch oven after the first 30 minutes of simmering.

### beef & mushroom pot pie
Prepare the basic recipe, adding 1 cup quartered button mushrooms, with the beef stock.

### beef & sausage pot pie
Prepare the basic recipe, browning 2 Italian sausages, sliced, with the beef. Return the browned sausage to the Dutch oven with the browned beef.

### beef & bean pot pie
Prepare the basic recipe, adding a 14-oz. can of red kidney beans, drained and rinsed, with the beef stock.

### beef pot pie with puff pastry
Prepare the basic recipe, replacing the basic crust with 1 sheet store-bought puff pastry. Brush the top with lightly beaten egg, leaving the edges egg-free to allow the crust to puff up. Make 4 to 6 slits in the top.

variations

# quiche lorraine

see base recipe page 150

### spinach & feta quiche

Prepare the basic recipe, omitting the bacon. Sauté 2 cups fresh spinach until the spinach wilts. Remove from heat and drain. Sprinkle 1/3 cup crumbled feta cheese over the base of the crust. Place the wilted spinach over the feta. Pour the egg mixture over the spinach and feta and proceed.

### ham & gruyère quiche

Prepare the basic recipe, replacing the bacon with 1 cup diced, cooked ham. Sprinkle 2 cups grated Gruyère or other Swiss cheese over the ham. Proceed.

### mushroom & thyme quiche

Prepare the basic recipe, omitting the bacon. Sauté 2 cups sliced mushrooms until they are tender. Sprinkle with 2 teaspoons chopped fresh thyme and sauté for 1 minute. Place the mushrooms over the base of the crust. Pour in the egg mixture and sprinkle with another 2 teaspoons chopped fresh thyme. Proceed with the recipe.

### cheese & onion quiche

Prepare the basic recipe, omitting the bacon. Sauté 1 yellow onion, sliced thinly, until soft. Spread the onion over the base of the crust. Sprinkle 2 cups grated Gruyère over the onion. Proceed with the recipe.

variations

# mixed mushroom tart with gruyère & pine nuts

see base recipe page 153

### mixed mushroom tart in whole-wheat crust
Prepare the basic recipe, replacing the basic crust with 1/2 recipe whole-wheat crust variation (page 19).

### mixed mushroom tart with thyme
Prepare the basic recipe, adding 2 teaspoons chopped fresh thyme leaves to the mushrooms as they are frying.

### mixed mushroom & onion tart
Prepare the basic recipe, adding 1 small red onion, sliced, to the mushrooms in the skillet.

### mixed mushroom tart on puff pastry
Prepare the basic recipe, replacing the basic crust with 1 sheet store-bought puff pastry. Roll out the puff pastry to a 13 x 9-in. (33 x 23-cm.) rectangle. Using a sharp knife, score a rectangular border, 1/4 in. (0.5 cm) from the edge of the pastry. Cut halfway through the pastry, taking care not to touch the bottom with the knife. Glaze the border with a lightly beaten egg. Do not prebake the puff pastry; simply fill and bake for 25 minutes.

# skillet fettuccini pie

see base recipe page 154

### spicy skillet fettuccini pie
Prepare the basic recipe, adding 3 small dried chipotle peppers. To prepare
the peppers, soak in 1/4 cup warm water for 10 minutes, then chop finely.
Add with the tomatoes.

### skillet fettuccini pie with monterey jack
Prepare the basic recipe, replacing the mozzarella with an equal quantity of
Monterey Jack cheese.

### skillet fettuccini pie with tuna & black olives
Prepare the basic recipe, adding a 6-oz. can tuna, drained, and 12 black
olives (kalamata), pitted and chopped, to the sauce with the tomatoes. Break
up the tuna with a wooden spoon while simmering. Replace the ground
cumin with 1 teaspoon dried oregano.

### skillet fettuccini pie with mushrooms
Prepare the basic recipe, adding 2 cups sliced button mushrooms to the onions.

### fastest skillet fettuccini pie
Prepare the basic recipe, replacing the dried fettuccini with fresh pasta.
Replace the tomato sauce with your favorite prepared tomato sauce.

# curried garbanzo & currant phyllo pie

see base recipe page 157

### curried garbanzo & zucchini pie
Prepare the basic recipe, adding 1 small zucchini, diced, to the saucepan once the onion has softened. Cook until tender and add the rice. Proceed with the recipe.

### curried garbanzo & currant phyllo pie with brown rice
Prepare the basic recipe, replacing the 1/2 cup basmati rice with an equal quantity brown rice. Increase stock to 1 1/2 cups. Proceed with recipe.

### curried garbanzo & eggplant phyllo pie
Prepare the basic recipe, adding 1 small eggplant, peeled and cubed, to the saucepan once the onion has softened. Before adding the eggplant, toss the pieces in a small bowl with 1/2 teaspoon salt and set aside for 15 minutes. Rinse and drain before adding to the onion. Cook until tender and add the rice. Proceed with the recipe.

# carrot & mint custard tart

see base recipe page 159

### carrot & cumin custard tart
Prepare the basic recipe, replacing the dried mint with 1 tablespoon
ground cumin.

### carrot & nutmeg custard tart
Prepare the basic recipe, replacing the dried mint with 1/2 teaspoon nutmeg.

### carrot & coriander custard tart
Prepare the basic recipe, replacing the dried mint with 2 teaspoons dried
coriander. Garnish with fresh cilantro leaves.

### carrot & sage custard tart
Prepare the basic recipe, replacing the dried mint with 1 teaspoon dried
sage. Garnish with fresh sage leaves.

### carrot & parsnip custard tart
Prepare the basic recipe, replacing 1/2 lb. carrots with 1/2 lb. parsnips.
Proceed with the recipe.

# mini pies & tartlets

Certain pies and tarts work best in individual

portions, as the recipes in this chapter demonstrate.

With just the right balance of pastry and filling,

these mini pies and tartlets will keep you coming

back for more.

# seedless raspberry jam tartlets

see variations page 188

Made with store-bought raspberry jam, these tartlets are just as easy to make as they are to eat!

1 recipe basic crust (page 18)                    18 tbsp. good-quality seedless raspberry jam

Preheat the oven to 375°F (190°C).

On a lightly floured surface, roll out half the quantity of pastry dough. Using a 3-in. (7.5-cm.) round cutter, cut out circles of pastry. Gently push the circles into the cups of a 12-cup muffin pan.

Collect the scraps, roll out, and repeat. Roll out the second disc of pastry dough. Each disc should yield 9 tartlet shells, but if you prefer a thick crust, make fewer (6 per disc). Spoon 1 level tablespoon raspberry jam into each tartlet shell (jam should fill 2/3 of the tartlet shell) and bake for 20 minutes, or until the jam is bubbling and the crust is golden brown.

Transfer to a wire rack to cool. To remove the tartlets from the muffin pan, gently slide a knife down the side of each tartlet and ease out.

*Makes 18*

# butter tarts

see variations page 189

Reminiscent of pecan pie or treacle tart, these rich and irresistible treats will appeal to those with a real sweet tooth.

| | |
|---|---|
| 1 recipe basic crust (page 18) | 1 cup light brown sugar |
| 2 large eggs | 1/4 cup half-and-half |
| 1/3 cup unsalted butter, softened | 1 tsp. vanilla extract |

Preheat the oven to 375°F (190°C). On lightly floured surface, roll out half the quantity (one disc) of pastry dough. Using a 3-in. (7.5-cm.) round cutter, cut out circles of pastry. Gently push the circles into the cups of a 12-cup muffin pan.

Collect the scraps, roll out, and repeat. Roll out the second disc of pastry dough. Each disc should yield 9 tartlet shells, but if you prefer a thick crust, make fewer (6 per disc).

Whisk the eggs in a heavy-based saucepan. Whisk in the butter, sugar, and half-and-half. Place the saucepan over low heat and bring the mixture to a boil, whisking constantly. When the mixture reaches the boiling point, remove from the heat. Stir in the vanilla.

Spoon the mixture into the tartlet shells so each one is 2/3 full and bake for 20 minutes, or until the filling is set and the crusts are golden brown. Transfer to a wire rack to cool. To remove the tartlets from the pan, gently slide a knife down the side of each tartlet and ease out.

*Makes 18*

# mini chess pies ⏱

see variations page 190

These little custard tarts have a long history in the Southern states, and can be flavored in a variety of ways.

1 recipe basic crust (page 18)
2 tbsp. unsalted butter, softened
1/3 cup light brown sugar
1/4 cup granulated sugar
pinch of salt

2 tbsp. all-purpose flour
2 large eggs
1 cup whipping cream
1 tsp. vanilla extract
1 tbsp. yellow cornmeal

Preheat the oven to 375°F (190°C). On a lightly floured surface, roll out half the quantity (one disc) of pastry dough. Using a 3-in. (7.5-cm.) round cutter, cut out circles of pastry. Gently push the circles into the cups of a 12-cup muffin pan.

Collect the scraps, roll out, and repeat. Roll out the second disc of pastry dough. Each disc should yield 9 tartlet shells, but if you prefer a thick crust, make fewer (6 per disc). To make the filling, cream the butter, sugars, and salt with an electric mixer. When the mixture is fluffy, stir in the flour and the eggs one at a time. Add the cream and vanilla, and beat until well combined. Pour the filling into the tartlet shells so each one is 2/3 full and bake for 20 minutes, or until the filling is set and golden brown on top.

Transfer to a wire rack to cool. To garnish, sprinkle cornmeal on the tops of the mini chess pies. To remove the tartlets from the pan, gently slide a knife down the side of each tartlet and ease out.

*Makes 18*

# burned caramel custard tartlets

see variations page 191

Like a crème brulée in pastry, these little tarts crackle with temptation. Burning the sugar into caramel is made easy with a chef's blowtorch.

1 recipe basic crust (page 18)
1/4 cup granulated sugar
5 large egg yolks
1 1/4 cups whipping cream

1/2 cup whole milk
2 tsp. vanilla extract
1/4 cup light brown sugar or turbinado sugar

Preheat the oven to 375°F (190°C). On a lightly floured surface, roll out half the quantity (one disc) of pastry dough. Using a 3-in. (7.5-cm.) round cutter, cut out circles of pastry. Gently push the circles into the cups of a 12-cup muffin pan. Collect the scraps, roll out, and repeat. Roll out the second disc of pastry dough. Each disc should yield 9 tartlet shells, but if you prefer a thick crust, make fewer (6 per disc). Beat the granulated sugar and egg yolks until well combined. Set aside. In a heavy-based saucepan, scald the cream and milk (heat over low heat until almost boiling). Slowly strain the cream mixture through a fine sieve over the egg and sugar mixture, whisking constantly. Stir in the vanilla and pour the filling into the tartlet shells so each one is 2/3 full. Bake for 20 minutes, until the custard is set and the crusts are golden brown. Transfer to a wire rack to cool. Then refrigerate for 1 hour.

Sprinkle the surface of each tartlet with brown sugar. Using a chef's blowtorch, heat the sugar until it caramelizes and becomes blackened in spots. Take care not to burn the crusts. Return the tartlets to the refrigerator for 15 minutes to allow the topping to harden. To remove the tartlets from the pan, slide a knife down the side of each tartlet and ease out.

*Makes 18*

# apricot tarts with hazelnut crust

see variations page 192

These little tarts delight the senses with their combination of flavors and textures — delicate fruit sitting atop a creamy filling, encased by a crunchy shell.

1 recipe hazelnut sweet crust variation (page 21)
1 recipe basic pastry cream (page 23)
4–6 14-oz. cans apricot halves in syrup,
   drained

1/4 cup apricot jelly or strained apricot jam
1 tsp. water

Preheat the oven to 425°F (220°C). Place a cookie sheet in the oven.

On a lightly floured surface, roll out the pastry dough. Using a 5-in. (13-cm.) round cutter, cut out circles of pastry. Gently press the circles into 4-in. (10-cm.) individual tartlet pans with removable bottoms. Trim the excess from the edges, collect the scraps, roll out, and repeat. The dough should yield 16 tartlet shells.

Place the tartlet pans on the hot cookie sheet. Bake blind for 5 minutes. Remove from the oven and remove the paper and weights. Reduce the oven to 350°F (175°C) and continue baking for up to 5 minutes, until light brown. Transfer to a wire rack to cool.

Whisk the cooled pastry cream and fill the tart shells, smoothing the tops with a spatula. Place 2 to 3 apricot halves on top of each tart, round-side up. Warm the apricot jelly in a small saucepan over low heat. Add water and stir until smooth. Using a pastry brush, glaze the top of each tart.

*Makes 16*

# pomegranate mousse in puff pastry patties

see variations page 193

Pomegranates have recently been added to the list of superfoods. It's the perfect excuse to try out this dessert!

1 package puff pastry patties
1 1/2 tbsp. unflavored gelatin
2/3 cup water
1 cup pomegranate juice
1 cup granulated sugar

zest and juice of 1 lemon
3 large egg whites
1 cup whipping cream
seeds of 1 pomegranate

Prepare and cook the puff pastry patties according to package instructions. Transfer to a wire rack to cool. To make the filling, sprinkle the gelatin over the water in a small saucepan and set aside for a few minutes. Add the pomegranate juice and sugar. Cook over low heat, stirring constantly, until the gelatin and sugar have dissolved. Remove from heat. Stir in the lemon juice and zest and chill in the refrigerator for 30 minutes, or until the mixture thickens. Using an electric mixer, beat the egg whites until soft peaks form. Transfer to another bowl, clean the beaters and mixing bowl, and beat the cream until soft peaks form. Gently fold the whipped cream into the chilled pomegranate mixture. When the cream is incorporated, gently fold in the egg whites. Spoon the pomegranate mousse into the base of the puff pastry patties. Garnish with a sprinkling of pomegranate seeds and place the pastry lid over mousse. Refrigerate any remaining pomegranate patties for up to 3 days.

*Makes 6*

# fig & ricotta tarts

see variations page 194

Fresh figs have long been accompanied by ricotta and honey; here this combination is lovingly assembled in a tartlet shell.

1 recipe basic crust (page 18)
2/3 cup ricotta cheese, drained
1/3 cup sour cream
2 tbsp. confectioners' sugar

1 tsp. vanilla extract
8–10 fresh figs, sliced in rounds
1/4 cup honey

Preheat the oven to 375°F (190°C). On a lightly floured surface, roll out half the quantity (one disc) of the pastry dough. Using a 3-in. (7.5-cm.) round cutter, cut out circles of pastry. Gently push the circles into the cups of a 12-cup muffin pan. Collect the scraps, roll out, and repeat. Roll out the second disc of pastry dough. Each disc should yield 9 tartlet shells, but if you prefer a thick crust, make fewer (6 per disc). Bake for 8 to 10 minutes.

To make the filling, combine the ricotta, cream, confectioners' sugar, and vanilla. Whisk until smooth. Fill each tartlet shell with the ricotta mixture and arrange 2 or 3 fig rounds, overlapping, over the filling.

Warm the honey in a small saucepan over low heat. Using a pastry brush, glaze each tart.

*Makes 18*

# shrimp & avocado barquettes

see variations page 195

These tiny boat-shaped pastries make beautiful appetizers.

1 recipe basic crust (page 18)
4 ripe avocados, mashed (keep covered until
   just before serving time)
1 cup mayonnaise

1/4 cup fresh lemon juice
salt and freshly ground black pepper to taste
2 cups cooked baby shrimp
1/4 cup chopped fresh flat-leaf parsley

Preheat the oven to 375°F (190°C). To prepare the barquettes, roll out half the quantity (one disc) of the pastry dough on a lightly floured surface to form a 13-in. (33-cm.) square. Using a barquette mold as a guide, trim the pastry, adding 1/2 in. (1.5 cm.) on either side. Press the pastry into the mold and trim the excess from the sides. Collect the scraps and repeat. Repeat with the second disc. Each disc should yield 12 barquette shells. Arrange the barquettes close together on a cookie sheet lined with parchment paper. Bake blind on the middle shelf of the oven for 15 minutes. Take out of the oven, remove the paper and weights, and return to the oven for 7 minutes, or until the barquettes are golden brown. Transfer to a wire rack to cool. When the molds have cooled enough to be handled, remove the barquettes and cool completely.

Combine the avocados, mayonnaise, and lemon juice until well blended. Season with salt and pepper. Spread the avocado mixture in the base of each, top with a few baby shrimp, and garnish with chopped flat-leaf parsley.

*Makes 24*

# onion chutney tartlets

see variations page 196

Look for prepared onion chutney in specialty food stores. If you can't find it, you can substitute your own favorite chutney.

1 recipe basic crust (page 18)
2 cups prepared onion chutney

1 cup pitted black olives, sliced
1 cup grated Gruyère or other Swiss cheese

Preheat the oven to 375°F (190°C).

On a lightly floured surface, roll out half the quantity (one disc) of the pastry dough. Using a 3-in. (7.5-cm.) round cutter, cut out circles of pastry. Gently push the circles into the cups of a 12-cup muffin pan. Collect the scraps, roll out, and repeat. Roll out the second disc of pastry dough. Each disc should yield 9 tartlet shells, but if you prefer a thick crust, make fewer (6 per disc).

Bake for 10 to 15 minutes, until the crust is golden brown. Transfer to a wire rack to cool.

Spoon the onion chutney into the tartlet shells so each one is 2/3 full. Arrange the sliced olives over the chutney and top with grated Gruyère.

Bake for 5 minutes, or until the cheese has melted. Transfer to a wire rack to cool.

*Makes 18*

# chocolate–peanut butter tartlets

see variations page 197

With peanut butter, chocolate pastry, and smooth ganache, this dessert is not just for kids!

| | |
|---|---|
| 1 recipe chocolate sweet crust variation (page 21) | 1/2 tsp. vanilla extract |
| 1/2 cup smooth peanut butter | 1/2 cup whipping cream |
| 1/2 cup cream cheese, softened | 4 oz. unsweetened chocolate, finely chopped |
| 2 tbsp. unsalted butter, softened | 1/2 cup whipping cream |
| 1/4 cup granulated sugar | 1/4 cup peanut halves |

Preheat the oven to 425°F (220°C). Place a cookie sheet in the oven. On a lightly floured surface, roll out the crust. Using a 5-in. (13-cm.) round cutter, cut out circles of pastry. Gently press the circles into 4-in. (10-cm.) individual tartlet pans with removable bottoms. Trim the excess from the edges, collect the scraps, roll out, and repeat. One crust recipe should yield 8 shells. Place the tartlet pans on the hot cookie sheet. Bake blind for 5 minutes. Take out of the oven and remove the paper and weights. Lower the temperature to 350°F (175°C) and bake for up to 5 minutes more, until the crust has darkened. Transfer to a wire rack to cool. Cream the peanut butter, cream cheese, and butter using an electric mixer on high speed. Slowly add the sugar and beat until fluffy. Stir in the vanilla. In another bowl, beat the cream until soft peaks form. Fold the cream into the peanut butter mixture. Fill the tart shells 2/3 full with the filling. Cover with plastic wrap and chill for 2 hours. Heat the whipping cream in a small, heavy saucepan to boiling. Pour the hot cream over the chocolate in a heatproof bowl. Stir until the chocolate has melted and the ganache is smooth. Cool for 30 minutes. Spread over the tops of the tartlets and refrigerate for 2 hours, until the ganache is solid. Garnish each tartlet with one peanut half.

*Makes 8*

# seedless raspberry jam tartlets

see base recipe page 171

### marmalade tartlets
Prepare the basic recipe, replacing the raspberry jam with an equal quantity of marmalade.

### strawberry jam tartlets
Prepare the basic recipe, replacing the raspberry jam with an equal quantity of strawberry jam.

### peach jam tartlets
Prepare the basic recipe, replacing the raspberry jam with an equal quantity of peach jam.

### chocolate-hazelnut tartlets
Prepare the basic recipe, replacing the raspberry jam with an equal quantity of chocolate-hazelnut spread.

### chestnut purée tartlets
Prepare the basic recipe, replacing the raspberry jam with an equal quantity of sweetened chestnut purée (crème de marrons).

variations

# butter tarts

see base recipe page 173

### butter pecan tarts
Prepare the basic recipe, adding 1/2 cup pecan pieces with the
vanilla extract.

### butter raisin tarts
Prepare the basic recipe, adding 1/2 cup raisins with the vanilla extract.

### butter currant tarts
Prepare the basic recipe, adding 1/2 cup dried currants with the
vanilla extract.

### almond-scented butter tarts
Prepare the basic recipe, replacing the vanilla extract with 1 teaspoon
almond extract.

variations

# mini chess pies

see base recipe page 174

### mini lemon chess pies
Prepare the basic recipe, omitting the vanilla extract and adding
3 tablespoons fresh lemon juice and the zest of 1 lemon in its place.

### mini cinnamon chess pies
Prepare the basic recipe, adding 1/2 teaspoon cinnamon to the filling
with the sugar.

### mini chocolate chess pie
Prepare the basic recipe, adding 2 oz. cooled and melted semisweet
chocolate to the mixture with the cream.

### mini chess pies with candied violets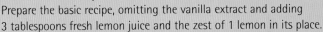
Prepare the basic recipe, garnishing each mini chess pie with
1 candied violet.

variations

# burned caramel custard tartlets

see base recipe page 177

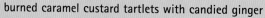

### burned caramel custard tartlets with candied ginger
Prepare the basic recipe, adding 1/4 cup minced candied ginger to the filling
with the vanilla extract.

### burned caramel custard tartlets with raisins
Prepare the basic recipe, adding 1/2 cup brandy-soaked raisins to the filling
with the vanilla extract.

### burned caramel custard tartlets with orange zest
Prepare the basic recipe, omitting the vanilla extract and adding 1 tablespoon
fine orange zest in its place.

### burned caramel custard tartlets with raspberry coulis
Prepare the basic recipe, serving each tartlet with a drizzle of raspberry
coulis (page 28). Garnish with fresh raspberries.

variations

# apricot tarts with hazelnut crust

see base recipe page 178

### apricot tarts with almond-scented pastry cream
Prepare the basic recipe, replacing the hazelnut sweet crust with the
confectioners' sugar sweet crust variation (page 21). Substitute the almond-
scented pastry cream variation (page 24) for the basic pastry cream.

### peach tarts with hazelnut crust
Prepare the basic recipe, replacing the canned apricot halves with canned
peach halves.

### apricot tarts with vanilla sweet crust & pistachios
Prepare the basic recipe, replacing the hazelnut sweet crust with the vanilla
sweet crust variation (page 21). Sprinkle 1 tablespoon chopped pistachios
around each apricot half before glazing the tarts.

### large apricot tart with hazelnut crust
Prepare the basic recipe, using a 9-in. (23-cm.) tart pan with a removable
bottom. Bake blind, and proceed with the recipe.

### apricot tarts with hazelnut crust & raspberries
Prepare the basic recipe, adding one fresh raspberry to the center of each
apricot before glazing.

variations

# pomegranate mousse in puff pastry patties

see base recipe page 180

### strawberry mousse in puff pastry patties
Prepare the basic recipe, replacing the pomegranate juice with 1 cup
strawberry purée. Make strawberry purée by processing 2 cups strawberries,
in either a blender or a food processor. Proceed with recipe.

### raspberry mousse in puff pastry patties
Prepare the basic recipe, replacing the pomegranate juice with 1 cup
raspberry purée. Make raspberry purée by processing 2 cups raspberries, in
either a blender or a food processor. Strain the pulp through a fine sieve or
food mill to eliminate seeds. Proceed with the recipe.

### chocolate mousse in puff pastry patties
Prepare the basic recipe, replacing the pomegranate mousse with the
chocolate mousse filling from Chocolate Strata Pie (page 120).

### lemon mousse in puff pastry patties
Prepare the basic recipe, replacing the pomegranate mousse with the lemon
mousse filling from Lemon Mousse Pie (page 93).

### coffee mousse in puff pastry patties
Prepare the basic recipe, replacing the pomegranate juice with
1 cup strong brewed coffee.

variations

# fig & ricotta tarts

see base recipe page 181

### fig & ricotta tarts with chopped pistachios
Prepare the basic recipe, garnishing each tart with 1 teaspoon chopped pistachio nuts before glazing with honey.

### fig & ricotta tarts with rosewater
Prepare the basic recipe, adding 1 teaspoon rosewater to the honey as it warms. Stir to combine. Garnish with edible flower petals.

### fig & mascarpone tarts
Prepare the basic recipe, replacing the ricotta cheese with an equal quantity of mascarpone.

### peach & ricotta tarts with lemon zest
Prepare the basic recipe, replacing the figs with 4 to 5 fresh, ripe peaches, peeled and sliced. Add the zest of 1 lemon to the ricotta mixture.

### fig & ricotta tarts with thyme
Prepare the basic recipe, adding 1 teaspoon finely chopped fresh thyme to the ricotta mixture. Garnish the glazed tarts with a few fresh thyme leaves.

# shrimp & avocado barquettes

see base recipe page 182

### shrimp & avocado barquettes with lime & cilantro
Prepare the basic recipe, replacing the lemon juice with an equal quantity of
lime juice. Replace the chopped flat-leaf parsley with chopped fresh cilantro.

### scallop & avocado barquettes
Prepare the basic recipe, replacing the baby shrimp with small
seared scallops.

### smoked salmon barquettes
Prepare the basic recipe, replacing the avocado mixture with 2 cups whipped
cream cheese. Top with strips of smoked salmon and garnish with thinly
sliced red onions and capers.

### smoked haddock barquettes
Prepare the basic recipe, replacing the avocado mixture with 2 cups
whipped cream cheese. Top with flaked smoked haddock. Garnish with
chopped chives.

### crab & avocado barquettes
Prepare the basic recipe, replacing the baby shrimp with flaked
cooked crabmeat.

variations

# onion chutney tartlets

see base recipe page 185

### onion chutney tartlets with anchovies
Prepare the basic recipe, adding 1 can anchovies, drained and cut in half. Arrange 1 or 2 pieces of anchovy over the onion chutney before adding the olives and cheese.

### onion chutney tartlets in whole-wheat crust
Prepare the basic recipe, replacing the basic crust with the whole-wheat crust variation (page 19).

### onion chutney tartlets with raclette cheese
Prepare the basic recipe, replacing the grated Gruyère with a square slice of raclette cheese.

### onion chutney tartlets with pancetta & bocconcini
Prepare the basic recipe, adding cubed, fried pancetta. Arrange a few pieces of pancetta over the onion chutney. Omit the olives and replace the Gruyère with a slice of bocconcini.

variations

# chocolate–peanut butter tartlets

see base recipe page 187

### chunky peanut butter tartlets
Prepare the basic recipe, replacing the smooth peanut butter with chunky peanut butter.

### chocolate–peanut butter tartlets in basic sweet crust
Prepare the basic recipe, replacing the chocolate sweet crust variation with the basic sweet crust (page 20).

### chocolate–almond butter tartlets
Prepare the basic recipe, replacing the peanut butter with an equal quantity of almond butter.

### double chocolate hazelnut tartlets
Prepare the basic recipe, replacing the peanut butter with an equal quantity of chocolate-hazelnut spread.

# individual pies & turnovers

Many countries have their own versions of hand-held pies, and with good reason. Excellent fare for bringing on picnics or packing in lunch bags, these portable treats provide a delicious snack, be they savory or sweet.

# spanish empanadas

see variations page 216

All over Latin America you can find empanadas bursting with local flavors.

| | |
|---|---|
| 1 package frozen puff pastry, thawed | 1/2 tsp. crushed red pepper flakes |
| 2 tbsp. olive oil | 1 tsp. ground cumin |
| 2 medium onions, chopped | 1 tbsp. white vinegar |
| 2 tsp. smoked sweet paprika | 1/4 cup raisins |
| 1/2 tsp. hot paprika | 1/2 cup pitted green olives, chopped |
| 1 lb. lean ground beef | 1 large egg, lightly beaten |

Preheat the oven to 350°F (175°C). Heat the oil in a large skillet. When the oil is hot, add the chopped onions and sauté for 3 minutes, until the onions are translucent. Add both paprikas, red pepper flakes, cumin, and vinegar and stir until well combined. Add the ground beef and cook until the meat is browned. Drain half the fat from the skillet. On a lightly floured surface, roll out the puff pastry 1/4 in. (0.5 cm.) thick. Using a 5-in. (13-cm.) cutter, cut out circles of pastry. One package of puff pastry should yield 8 rounds.

Using a pastry brush, glaze the top edge of each circle with water. Spoon 2 tablespoons filling onto the lower half of the circle. Sprinkle each with raisins and olives. Fold the top half of the circle over, pressing the edges to seal. Crimp the edge by twisting the pastry inward, from one side to the other. This will prevent the juices from leaking during baking. Glaze the tops of the empanadas with the egg. Prick the crust with a fork near the seam to allow steam to escape. Place the empanadas on a cookie sheet lined with parchment paper, and bake for 25 minutes, or until the filling is hot and the crust is golden.

*Makes 8*

# cornish pasties

see variations page 217

These hearty steak-filled handheld pies became popular as a lunch food among the tin miners of Cornwall, England.

1 recipe basic crust, dough divided into 4 discs
   (page 18)
1 tbsp. vegetable oil
1 small onion, finely chopped
1 large russet potato, peeled and diced
1/2 small rutabaga, peeled and diced

1 lb. stewing beef, such as blade or chuck, diced
1/4 tsp. mace
1/4 tsp. English mustard powder
salt and freshly ground black pepper to taste
1 large egg, lightly beaten

Preheat the oven to 400°F (200°C). Heat the oil in a large skillet. When the oil is hot, add the onion, potato, and rutabaga and cook until the onion is soft, about 5 minutes.

Add the beef and brown evenly. Reduce the heat, add the mace, mustard, and salt and pepper, and cook for 30 minutes, stirring occasionally. Remove from the heat. On a lightly floured surface, roll out the 4 discs of pastry dough. Using a pastry brush, glaze the top edge of each circle with lightly beaten egg. Spoon 1/4 of the filling onto the center of the lower half of each circle. Fold the top half over, pressing the edges together to seal. Crimp the edges by twisting the pastry inward from one side to the other, so a little knob of crust sticks out from one end of the pasty. Place the pasties on a cookie sheet lined with parchment paper and bake for 10 minutes. Lower the temperature to 350°F (175°C) and continue baking for 35 minutes, or until the filling is hot and the crust is golden brown.

*Makes 4*

# jamaican patties

see variations page 218

These spicy beef turnovers are as much a part of Jamaican culture as hamburgers are a part of American culture.

2 cups all-purpose flour
1/2 tsp. salt
1 1/2 tsp. baking powder
1 tsp. curry powder
1/2 tsp. turmeric
1/4 cup unsalted butter
2/3 cup vegetable shortening

1/3 cup ice water
2 tsp. vegetable oil
1 small onion, finely chopped
2 garlic cloves, minced
pinch of cayenne pepper
1 lb. lean ground beef
1 tbsp. curry powder

1 tsp. dried thyme
1/2 tsp. turmeric
1/4 tsp. salt
1/4 tsp. freshly ground
   black pepper
1 cup water
1/2 cup fresh breadcrumbs

Preheat the oven to 375°F (190°C). To make the dough, combine the flour, salt, baking powder, curry powder, and turmeric in a bowl. Cut in the butter and shortening until the flour mixture has the consistency of damp sand. Slowly pour the ice water over the flour, stirring until it is moistened. The dough should stick together and form a ball. Divide the dough into two balls and wrap each in plastic wrap. Smooth each ball of dough with a rolling pin so it forms a flat disc that fills the corners of the plastic wrap. Chill for a minimum of 1 hour, or up to 5 days. To make the filling, heat the oil in a large skillet. When the oil is hot, add the onion, garlic, and cayenne. Cook until the onion is soft, about 3 minutes. Remove the onion mixture from the skillet and set aside. In the same skillet, brown the beef over medium-high heat, about 5 minutes, or until no pink remains. Drain,

and return the onion mixture to the skillet. Add the remaining spices and cook for
3 minutes over medium heat. Add the cup of water and bring the mixture to a boil. Add
the breadcrumbs and cook for 3 minutes longer, until the mixture thickens slightly. Remove
from the heat and cool. On a lightly floured surface, roll out half the quantity (one disc) of
the dough. Using a 5-in. (13-cm.) cutter, cut out circles of pastry. Collect the scraps, roll out,
and repeat. Each disc should yield 8 rounds. Using a pastry brush, glaze the top edge of each
circle with water. Spoon 2 tablespoons of the filling onto the center of the lower half of the
circle. Fold the top half over, pressing the edges together to seal. Crimp the edge decoratively
and make 2 slits in the top. Place the patties on a cookie sheet lined with parchment paper
and bake for 20 minutes, or until the filling is hot and the crust is crisp and golden.

*Makes 16*

# greek spanakopita

see variations page 219

This delectable vegetarian pastry is easy to prepare and always well appreciated.

| | |
|---|---|
| 10 sheets phyllo dough, thawed if frozen | 1/2 cup ricotta cheese |
| 1 tbsp. unsalted butter | 1/2 tsp. dried oregano |
| 1 garlic clove, minced | pinch of nutmeg |
| 1 lb. baby spinach | salt and freshly ground black pepper to taste |
| 2 cups feta cheese, crumbled | 1/2 cup unsalted butter, melted |

Preheat the oven to 375°F (190°C). Melt the butter in a large skillet. Add the garlic and spinach. Sauté until the spinach is tender and wilts, about 5 minutes, then remove from the heat. When the spinach has cooled slightly, place in a sieve lined with a paper towel and press lightly to strain. Remove as much liquid as possible. Chop the spinach and transfer to a bowl. Add the cheeses, oregano, and nutmeg and stir to combine. Season with salt and pepper. Place the thawed phyllo sheets on a work surface. Remove 2 sheets and keep the others covered with a lightly dampened paper towel. Using a pastry brush, cover 1 sheet of phyllo with melted butter. Layer the second sheet on top and brush with butter. Cut the sheets lengthwise into 3 long strips. Imagine the end of one strip as a square made up of two triangles. Place 1 tablespoon of filling on the top triangle of the square, and fold the bottom corner up to encase the filling and form a triangle. Continue folding the pastry along the strip, maintaining the triangular shape. Place the finished pastry seam down on a cookie sheet lined with parchment paper. Glaze with melted butter. Repeat until all the phyllo and filling have been used up. Bake on the middle rack for 25 minutes, or until the filling is hot and the pastry is golden brown. Transfer to a wire rack to cool.

*Makes 15*

# italian calzone

see variations page 220

Calzone is rather like a folded or stuffed pizza. These are gourmet, homemade pizza pockets!

3 1/2 cups all-purpose flour
1 tbsp. granulated sugar
1 tbsp. instant-rise yeast
1 tsp. salt
1 1/2 tbsp. extra-virgin olive oil
1 cup very warm water
1 cup ricotta cheese

3/4 cup 1/4-in. (0.5-cm.) cubes mozzarella cheese
2 tbsp. grated Parmesan cheese
1/2 cup cubed prosciutto
2 tbsp. finely chopped fresh basil
freshly ground black pepper

Preheat the oven to 450° (230°C). To prepare the pizza dough, combine 2 cups of the flour with the sugar, yeast, and salt. Set aside. Warm the olive oil and water in a small saucepan over low heat. Slowly stir the water and oil into the flour mixture until well combined. Stir in 1 cup flour. Add up to 1/2 cup more flour as necessary to make a firm dough. Turn onto a lightly floured surface and knead until the dough is smooth and elastic, about 10 minutes. Lightly grease a large bowl with olive oil. Place the dough in the bowl and cover with a clean paper towel. Set aside for 10 minutes. While the pizza dough is sitting, prepare the filling. In a large bowl, combine the cheeses, prosciutto, and basil. Add freshly ground black pepper to taste. When the dough has rested for 10 minutes, punch it down. Cut the dough into 4 pieces, shape each into a ball, and flatten to form a disc. Lightly flour each disc. On a lightly floured surface, roll out each disc 1/8 in. (0.3 cm.) thick, and 6 in. (15 cm.) round. Add flour

as necessary to prevent sticking. Using a pastry brush, glaze the top edge of the circles with water. Spoon 1/4 of the filling onto the lower half of each circle. Fold the top over and press the edges to seal. Crimp decoratively and make 1 to 2 slits in the top. Place the calzones on a cookie sheet lined with parchment paper and bake on the middle rack for 30 minutes, or until the filling is hot and the crust is golden brown.

**QUICK & EASY SHORTCUT:** Replace dough with 2 packages of store-bought, refrigerated pizza dough.

*Makes 4*

# cheese & onion puff pastry pies

see variations page 221

Caramelized onions and melted cheese encased in flaky puff pastry is pure comfort food.

1 package frozen puff pastry, thawed
1 tbsp. olive oil
1 large onion, finely chopped
2 large eggs, lightly beaten
1 cup ricotta cheese

1/2 cup grated mozzarella
1/2 cup grated yellow cheddar
salt and freshly ground black pepper to taste
1 large egg, lightly beaten

Preheat the oven to 375°F (190°C). Heat the olive oil in a medium skillet. Sauté the onion until soft and golden, about 10 minutes. Remove from the heat.

In a medium bowl, combine the eggs, cheeses, and onion. Season to taste. On a lightly floured surface, roll out the puff pastry 1/4 in. (0.5 cm.) thick.

Using a 5-in. (13-cm.) cutter, cut out circles of pastry. One package of puff pastry should yield 8 rounds. Using a pastry brush, glaze the top edge of each circle with water. Spoon 2 tablespoons of the filling onto the lower half of the circle. Fold the top half of the circle over, pressing the edges to seal. Crimp with a fork.

Glaze the pie tops with lightly beaten egg and make 1 to 2 slits. Place on a cookie sheet lined with parchment paper and place in the middle of the oven. Bake for 25 minutes, or until the filling is hot and the crust is golden brown.

*Makes 8*

# indian samosas

see variations page 222

These deep-fried savory pastries make wonderful appetizers or picnic food. They are delicious served with a fruit or vegetable chutney.

2 cups all-purpose flour
1 tsp. salt
1/4 cup unsalted butter, melted
1/3 cup plain yogurt
water, as necessary
2 large potatoes, peeled and diced
2 carrots, peeled and diced
1/2 cup frozen peas
2 tbsp. olive oil

1 medium onion, finely chopped
2 garlic cloves, minced
1/2 tsp. finely grated fresh ginger
1/2 tsp. mustard seeds
1/2 tsp. curry powder
1 tsp. salt
2 tsp. fresh lemon juice
2 tbsp. finely chopped fresh cilantro
3 cups vegetable oil, for frying

To make the dough, combine the flour and salt in a large bowl. Stir in the melted butter and yogurt. Gradually add enough water to make a firm dough. Turn onto a lightly floured surface and knead until the dough is smooth and elastic. To make the filling, place the diced potatoes and carrots in a medium saucepan filled with water. Bring to a boil and cook for 5 to 10 minutes, until tender, but not soft. Add the frozen peas for the last 2 minutes of cooking. Remove from the heat, drain, and set aside. Heat the olive oil in a large skillet. When the oil is hot, add the onion, garlic, ginger, mustard seed, curry powder, and salt. Sauté until the onion is soft and translucent, about 8 minutes. Remove from the heat. Add the potatoes, carrots, and peas. Stir in the lemon juice and cilantro. On a lightly floured surface, roll out the dough 1/4 in. (0.5 cm.) thick. Using a 4-in. (10-cm.) cutter, cut out circles of

pastry. Add flour as necessary to prevent sticking. The samosa dough should yield 8 rounds. Using a pastry brush, glaze the top edge of the circles with water. Spoon 1 to 2 tablespoons filling onto the lower half of each circle. Fold the top over and press the edges to seal. Crimp with a fork. Heat the vegetable oil in a heavy skillet or saucepan. When the oil is hot enough that a drop of water bounces on contact, immerse the samosas. Fry until golden and crisp, about 3 minutes. Drain well and serve hot.

**QUICK & EASY SHORTCUT:** Indian Samosas in Spring Roll Wrappers variation page 222.

*Makes 8*

# easy blackberry turnovers

see variations page 223

These yummy turnovers are so easy to make they may well become your favorite homemade breakfast treat.

1 package frozen puff pastry, thawed
1/2 cup blackberry jam
1 1/2 cups fresh blackberries

1 large egg, lightly beaten
2 tbsp. granulated sugar, for sprinkling

Preheat the oven to 375°F (190°C).

On a lightly floured surface, roll out 1 block of puff pastry 1/4 in. (0.5 cm.) thick, 12 in. (30 cm.) square. Using a sharp knife, cut the square into four 6-in. (15-cm.) squares. Repeat the step with the second block of puff pastry. One package of puff pastry should yield 8 squares.

In a large bowl, combine the blackberry jam and fresh blackberries. Using a pastry brush, glaze the edges of the pastry squares with water. Spoon 1/4 cup filling onto the center of each square and fold each one in half, diagonally, to form a triangle. Press the edges to seal and crimp with a fork. Glaze the tops with egg and sprinkle with sugar. Make 2 to 3 slits in the top of each.

Place the turnovers on a cookie sheet lined with parchment paper and bake for 25 minutes, until the filling is hot and the crust is golden brown. Transfer to a wire rack to cool.

*Makes 8*

# apple currant turnovers

see variations page 224

Currants complement the flavor of apples beautifully in these tasty turnovers.

1 package frozen puff pastry, thawed
4 large cooking apples, such as Golden
    Delicious, peeled and chopped
1/3 cup dried currants
1/3 cup apple jelly, warmed
2 tbsp. cornstarch

1/2 tsp. cinnamon
pinch of nutmeg
1/4 cup unsalted butter, for dotting
1 large egg, lightly beaten
2 tbsp. granulated sugar, for sprinkling

Preheat the oven to 375°F (190°C).

In a large bowl, combine the apples, currants, apple jelly, cornstarch, cinnamon, and nutmeg.

On a lightly floured surface, roll out 1 block of puff pastry 1/4 in. (0.5 cm.) thick, 12 in. (30 cm.) square. Using a sharp knife, cut the square into four 6-in. (15-cm.) squares. Repeat the step with the second block of puff pastry. One package of puff pastry should yield 8 squares. Using a pastry brush, glaze the edges of the pastry squares with water. Spoon 1/4 cup filling onto the center of each square and dot with butter. Fold each one in half, diagonally, to form a triangle. Press the edges to seal and crimp with fork. Glaze the tops with egg and sprinkle with sugar. Make 2 to 3 slits in the top of each.

Place the turnovers on a cookie sheet lined with parchment paper and bake for 25 minutes, until the filling is hot and the crust is golden brown. Transfer to a wire rack to cool.

*Makes 8*

# strawberry fondue turnovers

see variations page 225

These unforgettably decadent treats get their name from their melted chocolate core.

1 package frozen puff pastry, thawed
10 oz. unsweetened chocolate
4 tsp. unsalted butter
zest from 1 large orange

2 cups hulled and halved fresh strawberries
1 large egg, lightly beaten
2 tbsp. granulated sugar, for sprinkling

Preheat the oven to 425°F (220°C). On a lightly floured surface, roll out 1 block of puff pastry 1/4 in. (0.5 cm.) thick, 12 in. (30 cm.) square. Using a sharp knife, cut the square into four 6-in. (15-cm.) squares. Repeat the step with the second block of puff pastry. One package of puff pastry should yield 8 squares.

In a medium saucepan, melt the chocolate and butter over low heat. Remove from the heat and stir in the orange zest. Using a pastry brush, glaze the edges of the pastry squares with water. Divide the strawberries among the 8 squares, arranging them to form a little well in the center of each pile. Pour 1 to 2 tablespoons melted chocolate in each well. Fold each pastry square in half, diagonally, to form a triangle. Press the edges to seal and crimp with a fork. Glaze the tops with egg and sprinkle with sugar. Make 2 small slits in the top of each. Place the turnovers on a cookie sheet lined with parchment paper and bake for 10 minutes, until the crust is golden brown. Transfer to a wire rack to cool.

*Makes 8*

variations

# spanish empanadas

see base recipe page 199

### broccoli empanandas
Prepare the basic recipe, replacing the beef with 2 cups cooked broccoli florets and 1 cup ricotta cheese. Omit the raisins and olives.

### chicken empanadas
Prepare the basic recipe, replacing the beef with 1 lb. skinless, boneless chicken breast, cubed.

### pork empanadas
Prepare the basic recipe, replacing the beef with 1 lb. pork tenderloin, cubed.

### sausage empanadas
Prepare the basic recipe, replacing the beef with 1 lb. mild Italian sausage, removed from its casing and crumbled.

### spanish empanadas with hard-boiled egg
Prepare the basic recipe, adding 2 hard-boiled eggs, finely chopped, to the filling mixture with the raisins and olives.

variations

# cornish pasties

see base recipe page 201

### cornish pasties with carrots
Prepare the basic recipe, adding 2 peeled and diced carrots with the potato and rutabaga.

### cornish pasties with ground beef
Prepare the basic recipe, replacing the stewing beef with 1 lb. lean ground beef.

### cornish pasties with parsnips
Prepare the basic recipe, adding 1 large peeled and diced parsnip with the potato and rutabaga.

### cornish pasties with green peas
Prepare the basic recipe, adding 1/2 cup frozen peas to the mixture before filling the pasties.

variations

# jamaican patties

see base recipe page 202

### curried lamb patties
Prepare the basic recipe, replacing the ground beef with an equal quantity
of ground lamb.

### curried turkey patties
Prepare the basic recipe, replacing the ground beef with an equal quantity
of ground turkey.

### curried vegetable patties
Prepare the basic recipe, replacing the ground beef with 2 cups assorted
chopped vegetables, such as carrots, peas, and potatoes. Place the vegetables
in a large pot of water. Bring to a boil and cook for 5 minutes, or until all
vegetables are tender. Drain and add to the skillet with the onion mixture.
Omit the water and breadcrumbs.

### mildly spiced jamaican patties
Prepare the basic recipe, reducing the curry powder in the dough to
1/2 teaspoon. Omit the cayenne pepper from the filling and reduce the curry
powder to 1 teaspoon.

variations

# greek spanakopita

see base recipe page 205

### spanakopita with leeks
Prepare the basic recipe, adding 2 large leeks, cleaned, halved, and sliced
thinly crosswise, to the skillet once the butter has melted. Sauté for
3 minutes, then add the garlic and spinach. Proceed with the recipe.

### spanakopita with onion
Prepare the basic recipe, adding 1 large yellow onion, finely chopped, to the
skillet once the butter has melted. Sauté for 3 minutes, then add the garlic
and spinach. Proceed with the recipe.

### spanakopita with raisins
Prepare the basic recipe, adding 1/2 cup raisins to the filling once the
cheeses have been incorporated.

### spanakopita with potato
Prepare the basic recipe, adding 2 large potatoes, peeled, chopped, and
boiled until soft, to the filling once the cheeses have been incorporated.

### spanakopita with dill
Prepare the basic recipe, adding 2 tablespoons chopped fresh dill to the
filling with the other herbs.

variations

# italian calzone

see base recipe page 206

### italian calzone with pancetta
Prepare the basic recipe, replacing the prosciutto with 1/2 cup pancetta, cubed and fried.

### italian calzone with artichoke hearts
Prepare the basic recipe, omitting the prosciutto and adding 1/2 cup drained artichoke hearts patted dry, to the cheese filling.

### italian calzone with pesto
Prepare the basic recipe, spreading 1 tablespoon fresh basil pesto over the pizza dough rounds, leaving a 1-in. (2.5-cm.) border before adding the filling.

### italian calzone with sun-dried tomatoes
Prepare the basic recipe, adding 1/2 cup drained and chopped sun-dried tomatoes to the cheese filling.

### italian calzone with black olive tapenade
Prepare the basic recipe, spreading 1 tablespoon black olive tapenade over the pizza dough rounds, leaving a 1-in. (2.5-cm.) border, before adding the filling.

# cheese & onion puff pastry pies

see base recipe page 208

### cheese, onion & potato puff pastry pies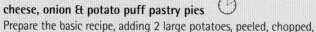
Prepare the basic recipe, adding 2 large potatoes, peeled, chopped,
and boiled until soft, to the filling with the eggs, cheese, and onion.

### cheese, onion & pesto puff pastry pies
Prepare the basic recipe, spreading 1 tablespoon fresh basil pesto over the
puff pastry rounds, leaving a 1-in. (2.5-cm.) border, before adding the filling.

### cheese, onion & sun-dried tomato puff pastry pies
Prepare the basic recipe, adding 1 cup drained and chopped sun-dried
tomatoes to the filling with the eggs, cheese, and onion.

### cheese, onion & mushroom puff pastry pies
Prepare the basic recipe, adding 1 cup sliced mushrooms sautéed in
1 tablespoon unsalted butter until soft and brown, to the filling with
the eggs, cheese, and onion.

### cheese & onion puff pastry pies with parmesan
Prepare the basic recipe, adding 1/2 cup freshly grated Parmesan
to the filling with the eggs, cheese, and onion.

variations

# indian samosas

see base recipe page 210

### indian samosas with beef
Prepare the basic recipe, adding 1 lb. lean ground beef, browned and drained, to the filling mixture.

### indian samosas with chicken
Prepare the basic recipe, adding 2 cups cooked, chopped chicken, to the filling mixture.

### indian samosas in spring roll wrappers
Prepare the basic recipe, replacing the samosa dough with store-bought spring roll wrappers. Fill each wrapper with 1 tablespoon filling. Using a pastry brush, glaze the edges with water and fold the wrapper in half to encase the filling and form a triangle shape.

### indian samosas with turmeric
Prepare the basic recipe, adding 1 teaspoon turmeric to the spices.

variations

# easy blackberry turnovers

see base recipe page 213

### apple-blackberry turnovers
Prepare the basic recipe, adding 2 large cooking apples, peeled, cored, and chopped, to the filling.

### raspberry turnovers
Prepare the basic recipe, replacing the fresh blackberries with an equal quantity of fresh raspberries and the blackberry jam with an equal quantity of raspberry jam.

### pear & blackberry turnovers
Prepare the basic recipe, adding 2 large cooking pears (Bosc or Anjou), peeled, cored, and chopped, to the filling.

### crimson turnovers (blackberry & raspberry)
Prepare the basic recipe, replacing half the fresh blackberries with fresh raspberries and half the blackberry jam with raspberry jam.

variations

# apple currant turnovers

see base recipe page 214

### apple date turnovers
Prepare the basic recipe, replacing the dried currants with an equal quantity of chopped dried dates.

### spiced apple turnovers
Prepare the basic recipe, adding 1/2 teaspoon cardamom to the filling mixture with the cinnamon and nutmeg.

### apple cranberry turnovers
Prepare the basic recipe, replacing the dried currants with an equal quantity of sweetened dried cranberries.

### apple raisin turnovers
Prepare the basic recipe, replacing the dried currants with an equal quantity of raisins.

### apple & dried cherry turnovers
Prepare the basic recipe, replacing the dried currants with an equal quantity of chopped dried cherries.

variations

# strawberry fondue turnovers

see base recipe page 215

### strawberry–rhubarb turnovers
Prepare the basic recipe, replacing the melted chocolate with
1 to 2 tablespoons stewed rhubarb in each turnover.

### double strawberry turnovers
Prepare the basic recipe, adding 1 teaspoon chopped dried strawberries
to the filling in each turnover before pouring on the melted chocolate.

### raspberry fondue turnovers
Prepare the basic recipe, replacing the strawberries with an equal
quantity of fresh raspberries.

### pear fondue turnovers
Prepare the basic recipe, replacing the strawberries with an equal quantity
of cooking pears (Bosc or Anjou), peeled, cored, and chopped.

### white chocolate strawberry turnovers
Prepare the basic recipe, replacing the unsweetened chocolate with an equal
quantity of good-quality white chocolate.

# cobblers, strudels & crumble pies

When you are craving pie but are short

on time, a cobbler is the obvious choice.

They are quick to assemble and just as easy

to eat. Crumble pies always delight with

their rustic charm.

# summer berry cobbler with vanilla-infused cream ⏱

see variations page 244

There's no better ending to a summer meal than a bowl of cobbler drizzled with cream.

1/2 cup granulated sugar
2 tbsp. cornstarch
pinch of cinnamon
2 cups fresh blueberries
2 cups fresh raspberries
2 cups fresh blackberries
1 1/2 cups all-purpose flour

3 tbsp. granulated sugar
1/2 tsp. baking soda
1/2 tsp. baking powder
1/4 tsp. cream of tartar
pinch of salt
1/4 cup unsalted butter, cut into small pieces

2/3 cup buttermilk
1 tbsp. granulated sugar, for sprinkling
1 cup whipping cream
1 tbsp. granulated sugar
1 vanilla bean

Preheat the oven to 425°F (220°C). Combine the sugar, cornstarch, and cinnamon in a large saucepan. Add the fruit, and stir to coat evenly. Cook over low heat until the sugar and cornstarch dissolve, about 3 minutes. Spoon into a buttered, deep-dish, 9 1/2-in.- (24-cm.) pie plate. To make the topping, combine the flour and next 5 ingredients in a large bowl. Cut in the butter until the mixture resembles coarse meal. Slowly mix in the buttermilk until just combined (mixture should be lumpy). Drop the mixture in mounds over the fruit, and sprinkle with sugar. Bake for 25 minutes, or until the filling is bubbling and the crust is golden brown. Place the cream and final tablespoon of sugar in a saucepan. Bring to a simmer over low heat, whisking to dissolve the sugar. When the cream begins to simmer, add the vanilla bean. Gently simmer for 5 to 10 minutes. Remove from the heat and remove the vanilla bean. Pour the vanilla cream over the servings of cobbler.

*Serves 6–8*

# fresh nectarine cobbler with citrus-scented crust ✒

see variations page 245

This quick-to-assemble dessert is simply ambrosial.

1 1/2 cups granulated sugar
2 tbsp. cornstarch
3 lb. nectarines (9 medium), pitted and cut into
    1/2-in. (1.5-cm.) slices
1 tsp. fresh lemon juice
1 1/2 cups all-purpose flour
3 tbsp. granulated sugar
1/2 tsp. baking soda

1/2 tsp. baking powder
1/4 tsp. cream of tartar
zest of 1 lemon
pinch of salt
1/4 cup unsalted butter, cut into small pieces
2/3 cup buttermilk
1 tbsp. granulated sugar, for sprinkling

Preheat the oven to 425°F (220°C). To make the filling, combine the sugar and cornstarch in a large bowl. Add the nectarine slices and lemon juice. Toss gently to coat evenly.

Place the fruit mixture in a buttered deep-dish (9-1/2 in. / 24-cm.) pie plate. Bake for 10 minutes, or until the fruit is hot. To make the topping, combine the flour and next 6 ingredients in a large mixing bowl. Cut in the butter until the mixture resembles coarse meal. Slowly mix in the buttermilk until just combined (the mixture should be lumpy). Drop the mixture in mounds over the fruit. Sprinkle with sugar.

Bake for 25 minutes, or until the filling is bubbling and the crust is golden brown.

*Serves 6–8*

# poppy seed strudel

see variations page 246

If you love poppy seeds, you won't want to miss this favorite Eastern European delicacy.

| | | |
|---|---|---|
| 1 cup all-purpose flour | pinch of cinnamon | 2 tbsp. honey |
| 2 tsp. baking powder | zest of 1 lemon | pinch of cinnamon |
| pinch of salt | 1-2 tsp. milk | 1/4 cup breadcrumbs |
| 1/2 cup unsalted butter, softened | 1/2 cup milk | |
| 1/4 cup granulated sugar | 1 cup poppy seeds, finely ground | |
| 1 large egg, lightly beaten | 1/4 cup granulated sugar | |

Preheat the oven to 375°F (190°C). To make the dough, combine the flour, baking powder, and salt in a large mixing bowl. Stir in the butter, sugar, egg, cinnamon, and lemon zest. Working quickly, knead the dough in the bowl, adding 1 or 2 tablespoons milk as necessary to make a firm dough. Cover and chill in the refrigerator for 30 minutes. To prepare the filling, heat the 1/2 cup of milk in a small saucepan. Add the poppy seeds and stir until the milk has been absorbed. Remove from the heat. Stir in the sugar, honey, and cinnamon. If the mixture is too wet, add breadcrumbs as necessary. The mixture should be smooth and moist. Turn the strudel dough onto a lightly floured surface. Roll out to a large rectangle, as thin as possible, about 15 x 12 in. (38 x 30 cm.). Cut the rectangle in half, making two rectangles about 7 1/2 x 12 in. (19 x 30 cm.). Spread the poppy seed mixture evenly over both halves. Roll up the strudels, tucking the ends under, to form two logs. Place the strudels on a cookie sheet lined with parchment paper and bake for 40 minutes, or until the crust is golden brown. Transfer to a wire rack to cool.

*Serves 6–8*

# quick chocolate banana strudel

see variations page 247

Be sure to use firm, ripe bananas to achieve the perfect balance of melted chocolate, smooth banana, and crunchy almonds.

4 sheets phyllo dough, thawed if frozen
3 tbsp. unsalted butter, melted
2 ripe bananas

1/4 cup semisweet chocolate chips
1/4 cup sliced almonds

Preheat the oven to 425°F (220°C). Place 1 sheet thawed phyllo dough on the work surface. Using a pastry brush, cover the phyllo with melted butter. Layer the other 3 sheets over the first, brushing each with butter.

Place both bananas together along one of the shorter sides of the rectangular pastry stack, leaving a 1-in. (2.5-cm.) border on all sides of the bananas. Sprinkle the chocolate chips over the bananas. Fold the borders over the bananas to secure them, and roll up the strudel.

Place the strudel, seam down, on a cookie sheet lined with parchment paper. Glaze the top with butter and sprinkle the sliced almonds on top. Cut 3 to 4 slits in the top of the strudel. Bake in the middle of the oven for 15 minutes, or until the chocolate has melted and the strudel is golden brown. Slice and serve.

*Serves 4–6*

# asparagus strudel with chèvre

see variations page 248

Make this strudel in the spring, when fresh asparagus is at its very best.

4 sheets phyllo dough, thawed if frozen
2 medium potatoes, peeled and diced
1 lb. asparagus, trimmed of rough ends and cut
    into 1-in. (2.5-cm.) pieces
1 cup soft goat cheese (chèvre)

3 tbsp. chopped fresh flat-leaf parsley
salt and freshly ground black pepper to taste
1/4 cup unsalted butter, melted

Preheat the oven to 400°F (200°C). Place the potatoes in a large saucepan, cover with water, and bring to a boil. Cook for 5 minutes, and add the asparagus. Continue boiling for 5 minutes longer, or until the vegetables are tender. Reserve 1/2 cup of the cooking water. Drain and set aside. Whisk the goat cheese until smooth and fluffy. Stir the vegetables into the goat cheese. Add a little vegetable cooking water if necessary to coat all the vegetables. Season with parsley, salt, and pepper.

Place 1 sheet thawed phyllo dough on the work surface. Using a pastry brush, cover the phyllo with melted butter. Layer the other 3 sheets over the first, brushing each with butter. Spread the asparagus mixture over the phyllo, leaving a 1-in. (2.5-cm.) border. Fold the border over the filling, and roll up the strudel. Place the strudel, seam down, on a cookie sheet lined with parchment paper. Glaze the strudel with melted butter. Bake for 25 minutes, or until the filling is hot and the strudel is golden brown.

*Serves 4–6*

# rhubarb crumble pie

see variations page 249

This pie is as pleasurable to make as it is to eat!

1/2 recipe basic crust (page 18)
1 cup granulated sugar
2 tbsp. cornstarch
zest of 1 orange
pinch of salt
6 cups rhubarb, trimmed of rough ends
    and cut into 1/2-in. (1.5-cm.) pieces

3/4 cup all-purpose flour
1/3 cup light brown sugar, packed
3 tbsp. granulated sugar
pinch of cinnamon
pinch of salt
6 tbsp. unsalted butter

Preheat the oven to 400°F (200°C). Roll out the pastry dough and line a 9-in. (23-cm.) pie plate. Crimp the edge decoratively. Chill in the refrigerator while you prepare the filling and topping. To prepare the filling, combine the sugar, cornstarch, orange zest, and salt. Add the rhubarb and toss to coat evenly. To prepare the topping, combine the flour, sugars, cinnamon, and salt in a medium bowl. Using your fingers, cut the butter into the flour mixture, until large clumps form.

To assemble, remove the piecrust from the refrigerator. Place the rhubarb mixture in the pie shell and sprinkle the crumble on top. Place the pie in the middle of the oven, and lower the temperature to 375°F (190°C). Bake for 1 hour. Check the pie; if the crumble is browned sufficiently, place aluminum foil over the top. Continue baking for 30 minutes longer. Transfer to a wire rack to cool.

*Serves 6–8*

# cinnamon plum crumble pie

see variations page 250

The combination of plums and cinnamon is utterly pleasing to the senses.

1/2 recipe cinnamon crust
   variation (page 19)
1/2 cup granulated sugar
3 tbsp. cornstarch
2 1/2 lb. plums (about 12), pitted and sliced
   thinly
3/4 cup all-purpose flour

1/3 cup light brown sugar, packed
1/2 tsp. cinnamon
pinch of nutmeg
pinch of salt
6 tbsp. unsalted butter

Preheat the oven to 425°F (220°C). Roll out the pastry dough and line a 9-in. (23-cm.) pie plate. Crimp the edge decoratively. Prick the surface with a fork and prebake for 15 minutes. Transfer to a wire rack to cool. Lower the temperature to 375°F (190°C).

To make the filling, combine the granulated sugar and cornstarch in a large bowl. Add the plums and toss to coat evenly. To prepare the topping, combine the flour, brown sugar, cinnamon, nutmeg, and salt in a medium bowl. Using your fingers, cut the butter into the flour mixture, until large clumps form.

To assemble the pie, spoon the plum mixture into the cooled piecrust. Sprinkle the crumble topping over the plums. Bake the tart for 40 minutes, or until the filling is bubbling and the crumble topping is golden brown. Transfer to a wire rack to cool.

*Serves 6–8*

# apple-caramel crumb pie

see variations page 251

Thick slices of apple coated in caramel make this dish lip-smacking!

1/2 recipe basic crust (page 18)
8 cooking apples, peeled, cored,
   and sliced thickly
1/4 cup all-purpose flour
1 1/4 cups granulated sugar

1/4 cup water
9 tbsp. unsalted butter
2 tbsp. water
3/4 cup all-purpose flour
1/3 cup light brown sugar, packed

1/2 tsp. cinnamon
pinch of nutmeg
pinch of salt

Preheat the oven to 375°F (190°C). Roll out the pastry dough and line a 9 1/2-in. (24-cm.) pie plate. Crimp the edge decoratively, and chill in the refrigerator. Place the apple slices in a large bowl with the flour. Toss to coat evenly and set aside. Combine the granulated sugar and water in a medium, heavy-based saucepan. Stir over low heat until the sugar has dissolved. Stop stirring, and let the mixture come to a boil. Boil for 10 minutes, occasionally swirling the liquid around the saucepan. When the mixture has turned dark amber, remove from the heat. Cool for a few minutes, then add 3 tablespoons of the butter and 2 tablespoons water. Swirl to melt the butter and combine. Return to the heat and stir until smooth. Pour the caramel over the apples and toss to coat evenly. Set aside for 10 minutes, while the apples release their juices. To prepare the topping, combine the flour, brown sugar, cinnamon, nutmeg, and salt in a medium bowl. Using your fingers, cut the remaining 6 tablespoons butter into the flour mixture, until large clumps form. To assemble the pie, remove the crust from the refrigerator. Spoon the caramel-apple mixture into the piecrust. Sprinkle the crumble over the apples. Bake the pie for 1 hour, or until the apples are soft and the crumb topping is golden brown. Transfer to a wire rack to cool.

*Serves 6–8*

# pear pie with pecan streusel topping

see variations page 252

In this recipe, pecans add crunch to the sweet streusel topping.

1/2 recipe basic crust (page 18)
3 tbsp. granulated sugar
2 tbsp. orange juice
pinch of salt
7-8 medium firm ripe pears, peeled, cored,
    and cut into small cubes
6 tbsp. all-purpose flour

6 tbsp. light brown sugar
1 cup all-purpose flour
1/2 cup light brown sugar, packed
1/2 tsp. cinnamon
1/4 tsp. salt
1/2 cup pecans, toasted and finely chopped
1/2 cup unsalted butter, cut into small chunks

Preheat the oven to 425°F (220°C). Roll out the pastry dough and line a 9-in. (23-cm.) pie plate. Crimp the edge decoratively. Prick the surface with a fork and prebake for 15 minutes. Transfer to a wire rack to cool. Lower the temperature to 350°F (175°C). To make the filling, combine the granulated sugar, orange juice, and pinch of salt in a medium saucepan. Add the pear chunks and toss to coat evenly. Cook over medium heat for 5 minutes, until the pears are beginning to soften but are keeping their shape. Remove from the heat. In a large bowl, combine the 6 tablespoons flour and brown sugar. Add the cooled pears and toss to combine. To prepare the crumble, combine the flour, light brown sugar, cinnamon, salt, and pecans in a medium bowl. Using your fingers, cut the butter into the flour mixture, until large clumps form. To assemble the pie, spoon the pear mixture into the cooled piecrust. Sprinkle with the pecan streusel and bake for 1 hour, or until the filling is bubbling and the streusel is golden brown. Transfer to a wire rack to cool.

*Serves 6–8*

# apricot tart with marzipan crumble topping

see variations page 253

Marzipan crumble adds a wonderfully rich texture to this sophisticated tart.

1 basic sweet crust (page 20)
1 large egg, lightly beaten
1/2 cup granulated sugar
3 tbsp. cornstarch
1 tsp. almond extract
2 1/4 lb. apricots (about 12), pitted
   and sliced thinly

3/4 cup all-purpose flour
1/2 cup light brown sugar, packed
1/2 cup almond paste (marzipan), packed
6 tbsp. unsalted butter
1/4 cup sliced almonds

Preheat the oven to 400°F (200°C). Roll out the pastry and line an 11-in. (28-cm.) tart pan. Prick the surface with a fork and chill for 10 minutes in the freezer. Bake blind for 20 minutes. Remove from the oven and brush the base of the tart with lightly beaten egg. Bake for another 10 to 15 minutes, until the edges are brown and the base of the crust is golden. Transfer to a wire rack to cool. Lower the temperature to 375°F (190°C). To make the filling, combine the granulated sugar, cornstarch, and almond extract in a large bowl. Add the apricot slices and toss to coat evenly. To prepare the crumble, combine the flour, brown sugar, and almond paste in a medium bowl. Using your fingers, cut the butter into the flour mixture, until large clumps form. Add the sliced almonds. To assemble the tart, sprinkle 3/4 of the marzipan crumble over the base of the cooled tart shell. Top with the apricot mixture. Sprinkle the remaining crumble over the top of the tart. Bake for 40 minutes, until the filling is bubbling and the crumble is golden brown. Transfer to a wire rack to cool.

*Serves 8*

variations

# summer berry cobbler with vanilla-infused cream

see base recipe page 227

### blueberry cobbler
Prepare the basic recipe, replacing the raspberries and blackberries with an equal quantity of blueberries.

### raspberry cobbler
Prepare the basic recipe, replacing the blueberries and blackberries with an equal quantity of raspberries.

### summer berry cobbler with whipped cream
Prepare the basic recipe, replacing the vanilla-infused cream with whipped cream.

### gooseberry cobbler
Prepare the basic recipe, replacing the berries with an equal quantity of fresh gooseberries. Increase the sugar in the filling to 1 cup.

### cherry cobbler
Prepare the basic recipe, replacing the berries with an equal quantity of pitted sweet cherries.

# fresh nectarine cobbler with citrus-scented crust

see base recipe page 229

**peach cobbler with citrus-scented crust**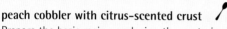
Prepare the basic recipe, replacing the nectarine slices with an equal
quantity of peeled peach slices.

**fresh nectarine & blackberry cobbler with citrus-scented crust**
Prepare the basic recipe, reducing the amount of nectarine slices by 1 cup
and adding 1 cup fresh blackberries.

**mango cobbler with citrus-scented crust**
Prepare the basic recipe, replacing the nectarine slices with an equal
quantity of peeled mango pieces.

**fresh nectarine cobbler with almond-scented crust**
Prepare the basic recipe, replacing the lemon zest in the topping with
1/2 teaspoon almond extract.

**fresh nectarine & cherry cobbler with citrus-scented crust**
Prepare the basic recipe, reducing the nectarine slices by 1 cup and adding
1 cup pitted sweet cherries.

variations

# poppy seed strudel

see base recipe page 230

### poppy seed strudel with raisins
Prepare the basic recipe, adding 1/4 cup raisins to the filling mixture.

### poppy seed phyllo strudel
Prepare the basic recipe, replacing the dough with store-bought phyllo sheets. To assemble, layer 4 sheets of phyllo, brushing each sheet with melted unsalted butter. Spread the filling over the sheets, leaving a 1-in. (2.5-cm.) border. Fold the border over the filling and roll up the strudel.

### poppy seed–orange zest strudel
Prepare the basic recipe, adding the zest of 1 small orange to the filling mixture.

### walnut strudel
Prepare the basic recipe, omitting the milk. Replace the poppy seeds with 1 cup finely chopped walnuts.

### walnut & raisin strudel
Prepare the basic recipe, omitting the milk. Replace the poppy seeds with 1 cup finely chopped walnuts. Add 1/4 cup raisins to the filling.

variations

# quick chocolate banana strudel

see base recipe page 233

### white chocolate banana strudel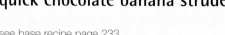
Prepare the basic recipe, replacing the semisweet chocolate chips with an
equal quantity of white chocolate chips.

### milk chocolate banana strudel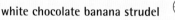
Prepare the basic recipe, replacing the semisweet chocolate chips with
an equal quantity of milk chocolate chips.

### butterscotch banana strudel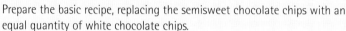
Prepare the basic recipe, replacing the semisweet chocolate chips
with an equal quantity of butterscotch chips.

### quick chocolate banana strudel with marshmallows
Prepare the basic recipe, sprinkling 1/4 cup miniature marshmallows
over the bananas with the chocolate chips.

### quick chocolate banana strudel with chopped walnuts
Prepare the basic recipe, replacing the sliced almonds with an equal quantity
of chopped walnuts.

variations

# asparagus strudel with chèvre

see base recipe page 234

### asparagus strudel with ricotta
Prepare the basic recipe, replacing the soft goat cheese with an equal quantity of fresh ricotta cheese.

### asparagus strudel with mint
Prepare the basic recipe, replacing the chopped parsley with 1 tablespoon chopped fresh mint.

### french bean strudel with chèvre
Prepare the basic recipe, replacing the asparagus with an equal quantity of crisp-tender French green beans.

### asparagus & prosciutto strudel with chèvre
Prepare the basic recipe, arranging 2 thin overlapping slices of prosciutto over the phyllo sheets before spreading with the filling.

variations

# rhubarb crumble pie

see base recipe page 236

### strawberry–rhubarb crumble pie
Prepare the basic recipe, replacing 3 cups chopped rhubarb with 3 cups hulled and halved strawberries.

### rhubarb crumble tart
Prepare the basic recipe, replacing the 1/2 quantity basic crust with 1 recipe basic sweet crust (page 20). Roll out and line an 11-in. (28-cm.) tart pan. Proceed with the recipe.

### rhubarb raspberry crumble pie
Prepare the basic recipe, replacing 2 cups of the chopped rhubarb with 2 cups fresh raspberries.

### rhubarb ginger crumble pie
Prepare the basic recipe, adding 1/4 cup minced candied ginger to the rhubarb filling.

### rhubarb apricot crumble pie
Prepare the basic recipe, adding 1/4 cup chopped dried apricots to the rhubarb filling.

variations

# cinnamon plum crumble pie

see base recipe page 237

### plum crumble pie

Prepare the basic recipe, replacing the 1/2 recipe cinnamon crust variation with 1/2 recipe basic crust (page 18).

### peach crumble pie

Prepare the basic recipe, replacing the plum slices with an equal quantity of peach slices.

### plum pie with marzipan crumble

Prepare the basic recipe, replacing the crumble with the marzipan crumble from the Apricot Tart with Marzipan Crumble Topping recipe (page 243).

### cinnamon plum & pear crumble pie

Prepare the basic recipe, reducing the quantity of plums to 1 1/2 lb. and adding 1 lb. pears, peeled, cored, and sliced, to the filling.

### plum crumble tart with almond sweet crust

Prepare the basic recipe, replacing the 1/2 recipe cinnamon crust with 1 recipe almond sweet crust variation (page 21). Preheat the oven to 400°F (200°C). Roll out the crust and line an 11-in. (28-cm.) tart pan. Chill in the freezer for 10 minutes. Bake blind for 15 minutes, then continue baking for 10 minutes. Transfer to a wire rack to cool. Proceed with the recipe.

# apple-caramel crumb pie

see base recipe page 239

### apple-raisin caramel crumb pie
Prepare the basic recipe, adding 1/2 cup raisins to the apple caramel mixture.

### apple-caramel pie with pecan streusel topping
Prepare the basic recipe, replacing the crumb topping with the pecan streusel topping from the Pear Pie with Pecan Streusel Topping recipe (page 240).

### apple-caramel crumb tart
Prepare the basic recipe, replacing the 1/2 recipe basic crust with 1 recipe basic sweet crust. Roll out crust and line an 11-in. (28-cm.) tart pan. Chill in the refrigerator while you prepare the filling. Proceed with the recipe.

### apple-caramel crumb pie with cheddar crust
Prepare the basic recipe, replacing the 1/2 recipe basic crust with 1/2 recipe cheddar crust variation (page 19).

variations

# pear pie with pecan streusel topping

see base recipe page 240

### plum pie with pecan streusel topping
Prepare the basic recipe, replacing the pears with an equal quantity of sliced pitted plums.

### pear & blueberry pie with pecan streusel topping
Prepare the basic recipe, adding 1/2 cup fresh blueberries to the pear filling.

### pear pie with walnut streusel topping
Prepare the basic recipe, replacing the pecans in the streusel topping with an equal quantity of chopped walnuts.

### pear & blackberry pie with pecan streusel topping
Prepare the basic recipe, adding 1/2 cup fresh blackberries to the pear filling.

variations

# apricot tart with marzipan crumble topping

see base recipe page 243

### peach tart with marzipan crumble topping
Prepare the basic recipe, replacing the apricots with an equal quantity of peeled, pitted, and sliced peaches.

### nectarine tart with marzipan crumble topping
Prepare the basic recipe, replacing the apricots with an equal quantity of pitted, sliced nectarines.

### pear tart with marzipan crumble topping
Prepare the basic recipe, replacing the apricots with an equal quantity of peeled, cored, and sliced pears.

### apricot tart with confectioners' sugar crust topping
Prepare the basic recipe, replacing the basic sweet crust with the confectioners' sugar sweet crust variation (page 21). Proceed with the recipe.

### apricot–cranberry tart with marzipan crumble topping
Prepare the basic recipe, adding 1/4 cup sweetened dried cranberries to the apricot filling.

# special-occasion pies

Pies and tarts hold a long-standing place in many festive celebrations. Enchant your guests with one of these traditional offerings at your next holiday gathering.

# pumpkin honey pie 🥄

see variations page 272

Naturally sweetened with honey and molasses, this aromatic pie is always a favorite at Thanksgiving.

1/2 recipe basic crust (page 18)
3 cups pumpkin purée
3/4 cup honey
2 tbsp. molasses
1/4 tsp. ground cloves

2 tsp. cinnamon
1 tsp. ground ginger
1/2 tsp. salt
4 large eggs, lightly beaten
12-oz. can evaporated milk

Preheat the oven to 450°F (230°C). Roll out the pastry dough and line a 9 1/2-in. (24-cm.) deep-dish pie plate. Crimp the edge decoratively and chill in the refrigerator.

Using an electric mixer, combine the remaining ingredients in the order listed, and beat until smooth. Remove the pie shell from the refrigerator. Pour the filling into the pie shell.

Bake in the middle of the oven for 10 minutes. Lower the temperature to 350°F (175°C) and bake the pie for 45 minutes more, or until the filling is firm around the edges and slightly soft in the middle. Transfer to a wire rack to cool.

Serve with whipped cream.

*Serves 6–8*

# sweet potato pie ✎

see variations page 273

This is another wonderfully tasty Thanksgiving classic.

1/2 recipe basic crust (page 18)
2 cups peeled, cooked, and mashed
   sweet potatoes
3/4 cup light brown sugar
2 large eggs, lightly beaten
1 tsp. cinnamon

1/2 tsp. nutmeg
1/2 tsp. ground ginger
1/4 tsp. ground cloves
1/4 tsp. salt
1 1/2 cups whole milk
2 tbsp. unsalted butter, melted

Preheat the oven to 425°F (220°C).

Roll out the pastry dough and line a 9-in. (23-cm.) pie plate. Prick the surface with a fork and prebake for 15 minutes. Transfer to a wire rack to cool. For the filling, combine the remaining ingredients in the order listed using an electric mixer, and beat until smooth. Pour the filling into the pie shell. Bake in the middle of the oven for 15 minutes.

Lower the temperature to 325°F (160°C) and continue baking for 40 minutes, or until the filling is firm around the edges and slightly soft in the middle. Transfer to a wire rack to cool.

Serve with whipped cream.

*Serves 6–8*

# tourtière

see variations page 274

This mildly spiced meat pie is traditionally enjoyed by French Canadians on Christmas Eve.

1 recipe basic crust (page 18)
1 lb. lean ground pork
1 tsp. salt
1/4 tsp. freshly ground black pepper
1/4 tsp. nutmeg

1 1/2 tsp. cornstarch
1 cup water
1 tbsp. olive oil
1 small onion, finely chopped
1 garlic clove, minced

Preheat the oven to 425°F (220°C). To prepare the filling, combine the ground pork, salt, pepper, nutmeg, cornstarch, and water in a medium saucepan. Simmer over medium-low heat, covered, for 30 minutes. Remove the cover and continue simmering for 10 minutes, until almost all the liquid has evaporated. Heat the oil in a small skillet. When the oil is hot, sauté the onion and garlic until soft, about 5 minutes. Remove from the heat. Add the onion to the pork mixture.

Roll out half the quantity (one disc) of the pastry dough and line an 8-in. (20-cm.) pie plate. Fill the pie shell with the pork mixture. Roll out the second disc and place on top of the pie, pressing the edges to seal. Crimp the edge decoratively and make 3 to 4 slits in the top. Bake for 10 minutes. Lower the temperature to 350°F (175°C) and continue baking for 30 minutes longer, or until the filling is hot and the crust is golden brown. Serve hot.

*Serves 4–6*

# mincemeat tarts

see variations page 275

Mincemeat, with its distinctive mix of currants, apples, candied citrus peel, and spices, has become a favorite seasonal ingredient.

1 recipe basic crust (page 18)                     1 tbsp. confectioners' sugar
2 cups prepared mincemeat

Preheat the oven to 375°F (190°C).

On a lightly floured surface, roll out half the quantity (one disc) of pastry dough. Using a 3-in. (7.5-cm.) round cutter, cut out circles of pastry. Gently push the circles into the cups of a 12-cup muffin pan. Collect the scraps, roll out, and repeat. Each disc should yield 9 tartlet shells, but if you prefer a thick crust, make fewer (6 per disc).

Spoon 1 level tablespoon mincemeat into each tartlet shell (the mincemeat should fill 2/3 of each tartlet shell) and bake for 20 minutes, or until the mincemeat is bubbling and the tart crusts are golden brown.

Transfer to a wire rack to cool. Dust with confectioners' sugar before serving.

*Makes 18*

# eggnog chiffon pie

see variations page 276

This pie takes the classic Christmas drink and turns it into a divine dessert.

1 recipe basic crumb crust (page 22)
1 tbsp. unflavored gelatin
1/4 cup cold water
4 large eggs, separated
1/2 cup plus 2 tbsp. granulated sugar
pinch of salt

1 1/2 cups hot whole milk
2 tbsp. dark rum
1 cup whipping cream
1 tbsp. confectioners' sugar
pinch of nutmeg

Preheat the oven to 350°F (175°C). Roll out the pastry dough and line a 9-in. (23-cm.) pie plate. Bake for 10 minutes. Transfer to a wire rack to cool. Sprinkle the gelatin over the water in a small bowl. Set aside for several minutes to soften. Place the egg yolks in a medium heavy-based saucepan. Whisk until smooth. Add the 1/2 cup sugar, salt, and hot milk and whisk until well blended. Cook over medium heat, stirring constantly until the mixture begins to thicken. The mixture should be thick enough to lightly coat a spoon or whisk. Add the gelatin mixture and rum and stir continuously until the gelatin has dissolved. Chill in the refrigerator, stirring occasionally, for 10 to 15 minutes, until the mixture begins to thicken, leaving a mound when dropped from a spoon. Using an electric mixer, beat the egg whites until they become foamy. Slowly add the 2 tablespoons sugar and continue beating until stiff and glossy. Gently fold the egg whites into the gelatin mixture until well combined. Spoon the filling into the cooled piecrust and chill in the refrigerator until set, about 3 hours. To make the topping, beat the cream with an electric mixer until stiff peaks form. Beat in the confectioners' sugar. Garnish with a sprinkling of nutmeg. Refrigerate any remaining pie for up to 3 days.

*Serves 6–8*

# galette des rois

see variations page 277

This pie, also known as Twelfth Night cake, is traditionally served in France on Epiphany.

1 package frozen puff pastry, thawed
1/2 cup unsalted butter, softened
1/4 cup granulated sugar
1 cup blanched almonds, finely ground
1/2 tsp. vanilla extract

1 tbsp. rum
1/2 recipe (1 cup) basic pastry cream (page 23)
1 egg, lightly beaten
1 small ceramic trinket or large dried bean
1 gold paper crown

Preheat the oven to 375°F (190°C). On a lightly floured surface, roll out 1 block of puff pastry to form a 10-in. (26-cm.) square. Using a sharp knife, cut out a 10-in. (26-cm.) round, using a dinner plate as a guide. Repeat the step with the second block of puff pastry. Using a sharp paring knife, decorate 1 pastry round with "s" shaped cuts, like swirly spokes going from the center to the edge of the round.

To make the filling, combine the butter, sugar, ground almonds, vanilla, and rum. Stir until well blended. Fold in the pastry cream until well combined. To assemble, place the undecorated round of puff pastry on a cookie sheet lined with parchment paper. Spread the almond filling over the circle, leaving 1-in. (2.5-cm.) border. Using a pastry brush, glaze the border with lightly beaten egg. Place a trinket or dried bean somewhere in the filling. Place the decorated round of pastry over the filling, pressing the edges to seal. Glaze the top with lightly beaten egg. Chill in the refrigerator for 1 hour. Remove and bake for 25 minutes, or until the pastry has puffed up and is golden brown. Transfer to a wire rack to cool. Decorate with the gold paper crown.

*Serves 6*

# double chocolate tart with raspberry & grand marnier coulis

see variations page 278

If food is the way to one's heart then this is definitely the right choice for a romantic Valentine's dessert.

1 recipe chocolate sweet crust variation (page 21)
1 large egg, lightly beaten
4 oz. unsweetened baking chocolate
1/4 cup unsalted butter
1 cup granulated sugar
3 tbsp. cornstarch
3 large eggs
1 1/2 tsp. vanilla extract

1 cup whipping cream
3 cups fresh raspberries
1/2 cup superfine sugar
1 cup fresh orange juice
zest of 1 orange
1/2 cup water
1/3 cup Grand Marnier or other
    orange liqueur

Preheat the oven to 400°F (200°C). Roll out the pastry and line an 11-in. (28-cm.) tart pan. Prick the surface with a fork and chill for 10 minutes in the freezer. Bake blind for 20 minutes. Remove from the oven and brush the tart base with lightly beaten egg. Return to the oven for 10 to 15 minutes, until the crust is set. Transfer to a wire rack to cool. Melt the chocolate and butter in a double boiler. Remove from the heat. Combine the sugar and cornstarch, add to the chocolate mixture, and stir until smooth. Using an electric mixer, beat the eggs until they become light yellow and thick. Stir into the chocolate mixture and return to medium heat. Cook for 5 minutes, stirring, until the mixture thickens and becomes glossy.

Whisk in the vanilla. Remove from the heat and cool completely. Using an electric mixer, beat the cream until stiff. Gently fold the chocolate mixture into the cream. Spread the chocolate filling evenly over the piecrust. Cover with plastic wrap and refrigerate for 4 hours. Place the raspberries, sugar, and orange juice in a saucepan and simmer for 15 minutes. Add the orange zest and water. Continue simmering for another 15 minutes, stirring occasionally. Strain the raspberry mixture through a fine sieve to remove the seeds. Stir in the liqueur and cool to room temperature. Drizzle the coulis over each slice of the tart and around the plate.

*Serves 6*

# sweet ricotta tart

see variations page 279

Variations of this tart are prepared all over Italy in celebration of Easter.

1 3/4 cups all-purpose flour
1/2 cup confectioners' sugar
1/2 tsp. salt
1/2 tsp. baking powder
zest of 1 lemon
1/2 cup unsalted butter, cut into small pieces
2 large eggs, lightly beaten

2 cups ricotta cheese
1/3 cup cream cheese, softened
1 tbsp. cornstarch
1 tsp. vanilla extract
2 large eggs, lightly beaten
1/2 cup superfine sugar
zest of 1 lemon

Preheat the oven to 350°F (175°C). To make the piecrust, combine the flour, sugar, salt, baking powder, and lemon zest in a large bowl. Cut the butter into the flour mixture, until the mixture resembles coarse meal. Add the eggs and stir until the mixture begins to form large clumps. Turn out onto a lightly floured surface and knead until the pastry is smooth, about 1 minute. Divide the pastry into 2 discs, one slightly larger. Wrap the smaller disc in plastic wrap and refrigerate. Press the larger disc around the base and up the sides of a 9-in. (23-cm.) tart pan. To make the filling, place the cheeses, cornstarch, and vanilla in a large bowl. Using an electric mixer, beat on medium speed until smooth. Add the eggs, sugar, and lemon zest. Beat until well combined. Spoon the filling into the tart shell, and smooth the top with a spatula. Remove the smaller pastry disc from the refrigerator. Place on a lightly floured surface and roll out to a 10-in. (26-cm.) round. Place the round over the cheese filling, trim the excess from the edges, and make 4 slits in the top. Bake in the middle of the oven for an hour, or until the pastry has puffed up and is golden brown.

*Serves 6*

# red, white & blue tart

see variations page 280

Bake this beautiful tart to celebrate Independence Day. Change the name to Tart Bleu, Blanc, et Rouge and you can celebrate Bastille Day on the 14th of July too!

1 recipe basic sweet crust (page 20)
1 large egg, lightly beaten
1 recipe basic pastry cream (page 23)

1 cup fresh raspberries
1 cup fresh blueberries

Preheat the oven to 400°F (200°C).

Roll out the pastry and line a 9-in. (23-cm.) tart pan. Prick the surface with a fork and chill for 10 minutes in the freezer.

Bake blind for 20 minutes. Remove from the oven, and brush the base of the tart with lightly beaten egg. Return to the oven for 10 to 15 minutes, until the edges are brown and the base of crust is golden. Transfer to a wire rack to cool.

Assemble the tart as close to serving time as possible. Whisk the cooled pastry cream and fill the tart shell, smoothing the top with a spatula.

Carefully arrange the raspberries and blueberries in a decorative pattern over the pastry cream, leaving gaps so that the pastry cream is not completely covered.

*Serves 6*

# marbled chocolate pumpkin cheese pie

see variations page 281

No need for trick or treating . . . just bake this exquisite pie in celebration of Halloween.

1 recipe chocolate wafer crumb crust variation
   (page 22)
2 cups cream cheese, softened (two 8-oz.
   packages)
2 tbsp. granulated sugar
1 cup pumpkin purée
3 large eggs, lightly beaten

3 tbsp. all-purpose flour
1 tsp. cinnamon
1/2 tsp. ground ginger
pinch of ground cloves
pinch of nutmeg
1/4 tsp. salt
1/2 cup semisweet chocolate chips

Preheat the oven to 350°F (175°C). Press the crumb crust into a 9-in. (23-cm.) pie plate and bake for 10 minutes. Transfer to a wire rack to cool. To make the filling, place the softened cream cheese in a bowl. Using an electric mixer, beat until smooth and fluffy. Add the sugar, pumpkin, eggs, flour, spices, and salt, and beat until well combined. In a double boiler melt the chocolate chips over low heat. Remove from the heat as soon as the chocolate is melted. Stir in 1 cup pumpkin mixture until well blended. Pour the remaining pumpkin mixture into the cooled crust. Drop the chocolate–pumpkin mixture on top, 1 tablespoon at a time. Drag the blade of a knife through the chocolate puddles, swirling to create a marbled effect. Bake for 45 minutes, or until the filling is firmly set around the edges, but still slightly soft in the middle. Transfer to a wire rack to cool. Chill completely in the refrigerator. For ease of slicing, wipe the knife with a clean, damp paper towel in between each cut. Refrigerate any remaining pie for up to 3 days.

*Serves 8*

variations

# pumpkin honey pie

see base recipe page 255

### pumpkin maple pie
Prepare the basic recipe, replacing the honey with an equal quantity of maple syrup.

### pumpkin pecan pie
Prepare the basic recipe, adding 1 cup pecan halves to the filling.

### pumpkin pie in whole-wheat crust
Prepare the basic recipe, replacing the 1/2 recipe basic crust with 1/2 recipe whole-wheat crust variation (page 19).

### pumpkin pie in gingersnap crumb crust
Prepare the basic recipe, replacing the 1/2 recipe basic crust with 1 recipe gingersnap crumb crust variation (page 22).

### pumpkin pie with spiked whipped cream
Prepare the basic recipe, garnishing the pie with spiked whipped cream (page 25).

# sweet potato pie

see base recipe page 257

### sweet potato pie in whole-wheat crust
Prepare the basic recipe, replacing the 1/2 recipe basic crust with 1/2 recipe whole-wheat crust variation (page 19).

### sweet potato pie with dates and orange
Prepare the basic recipe, adding 1/2 cup finely chopped dates and the zest of 1 orange to the filling.

### sweet potato pie with pecan crunch topping
Prepare the basic recipe, sprinkling pecan crunch topping (page 28) over the filling 30 minutes before the pie comes out of the oven.

### sweet potato tart
Prepare the basic recipe, replacing the 1/2 recipe basic crust with 1 recipe basic sweet crust (page 20). Roll out the crust and line an 11-in. (28-cm.) tart pan. Chill in the freezer for 10 minutes. Bake blind in a preheated 400°F (200°C) oven for 15 minutes. Remove the parchment paper and weights and continue baking for 10 minutes. Transfer to a wire rack to cool. Proceed with the recipe.

variations

# tourtière

see base recipe page 258

### ground beef tourtière
Prepare the basic recipe, replacing the ground pork with an equal quantity of ground beef.

### ground turkey tourtière
Prepare the basic recipe, replacing the ground pork with an equal quantity of ground turkey.

### millet tourtière
Prepare the basic recipe, replacing the ground pork with an equal quantity of cooked millet (see package for cooking instructions).

### vegetarian tourtière
Prepare the basic recipe, replacing the ground pork with an equal quantity of prepared textured vegetable protein.

# mincemeat tarts

see base recipe page 259

### mini mincemeat pies

Prepare the basic recipe, replacing the 3-in. (7.5-cm.) cutter with a 2-in. (5-cm.) round cutter. Gently push the circles into a 24-cup mini muffin pan and fill each 2/3 full with mincemeat. Bake at 400°F (200°C) for 20 minutes.

### mincemeat tarts with grated apple

Prepare the basic recipe, adding 1 freshly grated apple to the mincemeat.

### mincemeat tarts with hard sauce

Prepare the basic recipe. To make the hard sauce, beat 1 cup softened unsalted butter with 2 cups confectioners' sugar and 3 tablespoons brandy.

### mincemeat tarts with star-shaped lids

Prepare the basic recipe, cutting star shapes from leftover pastry with a 2-in. (5-cm.) star cutter. Place the stars over the mincemeat filling and proceed.

### mincemeat pie

Prepare the basic recipe. Roll out half the dough and line a 9-in. (23-cm.) pie plate. Fill with mincemeat and cover with top crust. Crimp the edge and make 3 to 4 slits in the top. Preheat the oven to 425° (220°C) and bake for 10 minutes. Lower the temperature to 350°F (175°C) and bake for 30 minutes more, until the filling is hot and the crust is golden brown.

variations

# eggnog chiffon pie

see base recipe page 260

### eggnog chiffon pie with rum-scented whipping cream
Prepare the basic recipe, topping the filling with rum-scented whipping cream. To prepare the rum-scented whipped cream, add 1 tablespoon rum to the whipping cream and confectioners' sugar.

### eggnog chiffon tart
Prepare the basic recipe, replacing the prebaked basic crumb crust with a prebaked 11-in. (28-cm.) basic sweet crust (page 20).

### eggnog chiffon tart in vanilla sweet crust
Prepare the basic recipe, replacing the prebaked basic crumb crust with a prebaked 11-in. (28-cm.) vanilla sweet crust variation (page 21).

### chocolate eggnog chiffon pie
Prepare the basic recipe, replacing the prebaked basic crumb crust with a prebaked chocolate wafer crumb crust variation (page 22).

### eggnog chiffon pie in shortbread crumb crust
Prepare the basic recipe, replacing the prebaked basic crumb crust with a prebaked shortbread crumb crust variation (page 23).

# galette des rois

see base recipe page 263

### galette des rois with frangipane
Prepare the basic recipe, omitting the pastry cream and substituting a simple frangipane filling (almond mixture) as used in the English Bakewell Tart recipe (page 45).

### galette des rois with ground hazelnuts
Prepare the basic recipe, replacing the ground almonds with an equal quantity of ground hazelnuts.

### galette des rois with ground pistachios
Prepare the basic recipe, replacing the ground almonds with an equal quantity of ground pistachios.

### galette des rois with rum-scented pastry cream
Prepare the basic recipe, replacing the basic pastry cream with an equal quantity of rum-scented pastry cream (page 24).

# double chocolate tart with raspberry & grand marnier coulis

see base recipe page 264

### double chocolate tart with white chocolate filling
Prepare the basic recipe, omitting the sugar in the filling and replacing the unsweetened chocolate with an equal quantity of white chocolate.

### double chocolate tart with cranberry coulis
Prepare the basic recipe, replacing the raspberries with cranberries. Omit the Grand Marnier if desired.

### double chocolate tart with chocolate-dipped strawberries
Prepare the basic recipe, garnishing with chocolate-dipped strawberries. To make chocolate-dipped strawberries, dip fresh strawberries in 4 oz. melted semisweet chocolate, so that half the strawberry is coated. Place on a cookie sheet lined with parchment paper. Repeat until the strawberries and chocolate have been used up. Refrigerate until the chocolate has hardened.

### double chocolate tartlets with raspberry coulis
Prepare the basic recipe, omitting the Grand Marnier from the raspberry coulis.

### chocolate tart in almond sweet crust
Prepare the basic recipe, replacing the prebaked chocolate sweet crust with a prebaked almond sweet crust variation (page 21).

# sweet ricotta tart

see base recipe page 267

### sweet ricotta tart with orange
Prepare the basic recipe, replacing the lemon zest and juice with the zest and juice of half an orange.

### sweet ricotta tart with almond
Prepare the basic recipe, adding 1 teaspoon almond extract to the filling mixture.

### sweet mascarpone tart
Prepare the basic recipe, replacing the ricotta cheese with mascarpone cheese.

### sweet mocha ricotta tart
Prepare the basic recipe, omitting the lemon zest and juice. Dissolve 1 teaspoon instant espresso powder and 1 teaspoon instant hot chocolate powder in 2 tablespoons milk and add to the ricotta mixture.

variations

# red, white & blue tart

see base recipe page 268

### red, white & blue tart with cream cheese filling
Prepare the basic recipe, replacing the basic pastry cream with the basic cream cheese filling (page 24).

### red, white & blue flag tart (in rectangular tart pan)
Double the quantities of the basic recipe. Prebake the basic sweet tart shells in two 4 x 14-in. (10 x 35-cm.) tart pans. Dust the edges of the crust with confectioners' sugar. Fill with basic pastry cream and arrange the berries to resemble the American Flag. Continue the stripes in the second tart.

### bleu, blanc & rouge flag tart (for bastille day)
Triple the basic recipe. Prebake the basic sweet tart shells in three 4 x 14-in. (10 x 35-cm.) tart pans. Dust the edges of the crust with confectioners' sugar. Fill with basic pastry cream (page 23) and arrange the berries to resemble the French flag: Set the three tarts side by side and fill one with glazed blueberries; one with another variety of berry, heavily dusted with confectioners' sugar; and the last one with glazed raspberries.

### red, white & blue tart in vanilla sweet crust
Prepare the basic recipe, replacing the fully baked basic sweet crust with a fully baked vanilla sweet crust variation (page 21).

variations

# marbled chocolate pumpkin cheese pie

see base recipe page 271

### spider web motif pumpkin chocolate cheese pie
Prepare the basic recipe, drizzling the chocolate mixture in concentric circles over the pumpkin filling. Place one spoonful of the chocolate mixture in the center. Drag the blade of a sharp knife through the chocolate in straight lines, from the middle to the edge of the pie, like the spokes of a bicycle wheel, to create the spider web motif.

### marbled pumpkin chocolate cheese pie in gingersnap crumb crust
Prepare the basic recipe, replacing the prebaked chocolate crumb crust with a prebaked gingersnap crumb crust variation (page 22).

### marbled pumpkin chocolate cheese pie with shortbread crumb crust
Prepare the basic recipe, replacing the prebaked chocolate crumb crust with a prebaked shortbread crumb crust variation (page 22).

### marbled pumpkin chocolate cheese pie with crumb crust
Prepare the basic recipe, replacing the chocolate crumb crust with a prebaked basic crumb crust (page 22).

# index